RUGGED FAITH

52 STORIES OF FAITH, OUTDOORS, & LIFE

A WEEKLY READER
FOR GUYS WHO
DON'T READ MUCH!

JACK WARD
FOUNDER OF *RUGGED FAITH MINISTRIES*

Rugged Faith: 52 Stories of Faith, Outdoors, & Life

ISBN978-0-615-43232-8
Published by Rugged Faith Publishers
193 Niagara St
Springdale, AR 72762

Cover and page design by Lamb Creek Design
1207 Monroe Drive
Kerrville, TX 78028
www.lambcreekcom

First Printing: 2011
Printed by CreateSpace in the United States

This book is dedicated
to my son Ross,
who inspires me
to be a better man.

I love you, son.

Table of Contents

Foreword

There are men who are growing continually in their Christian faith but they seem to be the exception and not the rule. Why is that? How can a man be a member of a church that teaches the Bible week after week, month after month and still not grow and change? What is missing? After all, the Bible is God's Word and is 'alive and active, sharper than any double-edged sword, it penetrates even to dividing soul and spirit, joints and marrow; it judges the thoughts and attitudes of the heart' (Hebrews 4:12, NIV).

Many men go to church on Sunday. The man there who is teaching the Bible should understand men. He is a man and deals with many of the same issues and struggles that the men he is teaching deal with each and every day. The church is probably

40–50% men each Sunday so there are others who should be heading in the same direction. These men are automatically in some form of community with one another. Shouldn't ongoing regular community encourage growth and change among men?

The principles seem to be in place but the context is in need of an overhaul.

Men change and grow in the context of relationships. Men need to hear and embrace God's Word but they need to do it with other men. They need to hear and understand how God's Word is applied in another man's life. Men long to hear examples, illustrations, pathways, models and stories that show them what it really looks like to follow Christ and be God's Man in their different arenas of life.

Jack Ward understands this and that is why *Rugged Faith* is a collection of stories of men who are growing in Christ. Inside this book are those examples, illustrations, pathways, models and stories that let men see what it looks like to move forward as a follower of Jesus and to do this with other men.

I want to be that type of man. How about you? Grab another guy and enjoy this book together.

Brian Doyle

National Director

Iron Sharpens Iron

Introduction

Growing up in the Ozark National Forest, I came to love the sounds, smells, and sights of the outdoors. Thanks to my dad and my older brothers, I learned to hunt and fish the mountains and streams of Arkansas and developed a love for exploring.

This book and Rugged Faith Ministries are an exploration. To write about my life in the Leatherwoods and to serve a God that forgives and frees is an expedition more exciting than anything I have ever done.

Why God would allow me to carry His Word to men is still a mystery to me. I never quite feel worthy of God's grace.

I pray that these short stories will encourage you to dream big and to allow God to use you. He has created you with a special combination of talents and gifts necessary to carry out the plan He has for your life.

Take heart knowing that if God can use a wretch like me, He can use you if you are willing. Every day of your life can be filled with peace, joy, and purpose when you live with Rugged Faith.

As I write this I can't help but remember all those who have supported and encouraged me throughout the years. I remember my mother who struggled and prayed for me, my wife who loves and encourages me, and my son who inspires and pushes me to do better.

I want to thank Megan Blankenship and Nikki Connelly for advice and Dave Rogers at Lamb Creek for design. A Special thank you to Steve Perryman, Mel Reed, David Hartshorn, Ben Dallas, Danny Ponder, Mark Connelly, Norman Strawbridge, Dale Armstrong, Brian Doyle, and many other men who have supported and encouraged me to go further so God might get the glory.

1 Adventure

The little 14-foot aluminum boot bounces across the strong current of the Kenai River. Fishing boats swarm like Wal-Mart shoppers on Black Friday. Through the early morning mist the Kenai River is humming with life. This is my first day of fishing for the Alaska King Salmon.

The Kenai is a big river, deep, swift, and wide near its mouth on the Cook Inlet of the northern Pacific Ocean. Its turquoise, glacier-fed waters flow for 82 miles and have some of the best salmon fishing in the world.

Each year there are two runs of the kings, silvers, and red salmon. The world record 97-pound king salmon was caught here in 1985. I'm here with Rick, a buddy I have known since our elementary schools days in Arkansas. Rick and his wife Jan came to Alaska in 1975 during the oil pipeline boom.

Rick guides the little boat he calls "The Calypso" through the choppy waters and around the growing mass of fisherman. "This should be as good a spot as any," he yells over the roar of the motors. I cast my line into the frigid water and tug at the hood of my raincoat to keep the mist off my face.

This is different than any kind of fishing I have ever done. I have fished the rivers and streams of the Ozarks for trout and smallmouth bass, but this is my first attempt at big game fishing.

When God made Alaska He sure outdid Himself. It's like no other place in the world. Wild, untamed, and diverse, it screams, "This is God's Country."

Men are drawn to Alaska. Rick and his twin brother Meryl came here to work in the logging industry and on the oil pipeline.

The twins, like many other men, came to Alaska for the work, but they came more for adventure, the hunting and fishing, and the call of the wild.

After no more than 20 minutes of fishing I get a heavy tug on my line. "Is that a fish?" I ask Rick. "You got him, hang on," comes the reply as Rick fires up the 50 horsepower Johnson and maneuvers our boat into position to net the fish. It's a 41-pound king salmon, the biggest fish I have ever caught.

Adventures like this one and the ones to follow are what men live for. When we can blend adventure and Christianity into the lives of men, we have a much better chance of reaching them for Christ. When a man can see that church does not have to be boring and feminine, that a Christian man can be wild and adventurous like God made him, he can begin to find his God given purpose in life.

Rugged Faith attempts to model godly masculinity through all our events, teaching, and promotions. We want to assure men that God will bless His strong, bold followers. Once men realize that a Bible study with other men can be exciting and meaningful without being mushy or touchy-feely, they will grow deeper in their relationships with God and with other men.

2

A Worthy Walk

The crisp autumn air clears my head as Mark and I start up the first gentle incline on this section of the Ozark Highland Trail. The path is surprisingly well maintained, considering the recent ice storm.

All around us trees are bent and broken from the weight of the ice that caused such havoc in this area a few months ago.

The Ozark Highland Trail is worthy of your time and effort. It is one of the most spectacular hiking trails in the United States. This cross-country route stretches 165 miles across Northwest Arkansas.

It crosses more than 60 creeks, streams, and rivers and passes hundreds of seasonal waterfalls, giant cliffs, and scenic vistas.

Most of the trail is clearly marked with white, metal reflectors nailed on trees. Just when you think you are about to lose the trail, a distinctive marker appears on a tree up ahead.

Just as the Ozark Highland Trail was clearly marked by the hundreds of volunteers who build the route, the Via Dolorosa was clearly marked. This narrow street in ancient Jerusalem is the blood-sprinkled path our Savior walked, carrying His cross, on the way to His crucifixion.

Ironically, today the Temple Mount blocks the "Way to the Cross." This Muslim holy site was built across the ancient street known as the Via Dolorosa. The road now splits and goes around the Temple Mount.

The Ozark Highland Trail passes through some of the most remote and scenic portions of the Ozark Mountains. It passes areas like the Buffalo River, Hurricane Creek, Lick Creek, Potato Knob and Ozone. Today we are hiking a six mile section that skirts the White River near Lone Rock.

It's the fall of the year, and as we reach the top of a high ridge, we look out across the vistas and marvel at the brilliant autumn colors of the trees and thank God for a place such as this.

Today we enjoy this beautiful area because of the many dedicated volunteers who have worked to build, mark, and maintain this trail across the Ozarks.

All the blessings of creation are available to us because on that day over 2000 years ago Jesus walked "The Way of the Cross" in Jerusalem. He carried with Him the sins of the world. Burdened by a heavy wooden cross, He bled and died for your sins and mine so that we might have eternal life.

The way of the cross leads to God's best for our lives. The most satisfying steps in life are found when we walk in the shadow of the cross.

Colossians 1:10 tells us to "walk in a manner worthy of the Lord." A worthy walk has six steps. First, it pleases Him in all respects. We must walk in a way that is pleasing to God.

He wants us to walk in a manner, a style, a practice, a method according to our birthright as adopted sons of God, and as accustomed to or expected of one who is a child of a king.

This manner or style of walk should be pleasing to God. When we are obedient, loving, forgiving, and all the other ways of Jesus, we enter into a worthy walk.

Secondly, a worthy walk bears fruit in every good work. Is your walk bearing good fruit? Or are you walking through life for yourself? Are your good works done to impress others, or to introduce them to Jesus?

Third, a worthy walk increases our knowledge of God. If we are walking with God we will want to know more about Him. We will have a hunger for the things of God.

The next step is strength of character and steadfastness. When we walk in a way that pleases God, we will be strengthened by His power. We have met people who have strength of character which we all admire. To get there, these people have walked with God in these six areas. They have a steadfast life that has been built on the worthy Word of God; His thoughts are engraved upon their hearts.

The fifth step in a worthy walk is patience. This step does not happen overnight. Patience is developed over a long and steady walk with the Lord. It's so foreign to our sinful, selfish nature that it takes time, but it certainly is pleasing to God and worthy of His praise.

The final step in a worthy walk is thankfulness. When we are walking with Him, we are joyously giving thanks to a Father who has qualified us to be a part of His family. We share in the inheritance of those who have faithfully walked with God down through the ages.

As my friend Mark and I finish this section of the trail, we are winded, but invigorated. We are thankful for this opportunity to enjoy God's creation and thankful that we can walk with the creator. It's a worthy walk.

3
The Unknown

Outdoor adventure can give men the excitement of seeing what's over the next ridge or what's around the next bend in the river. The anticipation of the unknown can be an adrenaline rush.

What's next? Are there more steep trails ahead, or will the trail flatten out into a lush valley below? What will the next bend in the river reveal? Will it produce another great fishing hole or unexpected white-water rapids, hidden from our ears?

Following God in this great adventure called life is packed full of the divine unknown. Every day I smile and say, "Lord, what's next? Where do we go from here?" Will He lead me to someone who is hurting or troubled and expect me to say just the right words of encouragement? Is today one of those days when I will be tested with sexual temptation or thoughts of bitterness or anger that keep coming to the surface? Or will it be another one of those times when God pours out His blessings of opened doors that allow this ministry to expand, that allow me to build rugged faith?

Over the past year I have been riding this rush of the unknown. I never want it to stop. Each day it is new, exciting, and humbling to see God's works and see how He uses a wretch like me to accomplish far more than I ever thought possible.

The unknown can be safe and, at the same time, scary. Just knowing that God is in control, that He is my guide, puts me at peace and calms my fears, but when I take my eyes off my guide and begin to look back at where I have come from, or allow myself to think about what's next, I get a little bit spooked.

The trail ahead seems too steep and the river rapids start to look mighty rough. The clouds turn dark and the trees begin to press in around me. It can happen in a split second. I can be right in God's shadow one second and the next I can make a wrong turn and feel like I'm lost in the wilderness of life.

He does take me to places I would have never imagined just a few months ago. Places and people and opportunities that I once only dreamed of are now the norm. Problems, hurts, and disappointments that just a year ago would have made me quit now seem like gifts that help me grow.

Chance meetings and coincidences of the past are now more than accidents. These opportunities are steps to building rugged faith in a life that once had no purpose. Most of my life has been "accident-driven" instead of purpose-driven. I have bounced from one thing to the next never being satisfied for more than a few hours or days.

The unknown was a hill to conquer. So I would make a run at it and if I made it to the top, I would coast down the other side. If I didn't make it to the top, I just blamed someone and stomped off to find another hill.

This "Unknown" is different. God takes me along with Him. He chooses which hills we tackle and He picks a time when He knows I'm ready. Following His lead is a humble blessing when I look at my past and compare my life to a perfect and holy God.

At our boot camps the unknown is everywhere. Will anyone show up? Will the men who attend get their money's worth? The responses we receive from men who do attend these events always surprise me. We never know what is going to touch a heart. It can be something as odd as a comment or illustration from one of the speakers or as routine as a morning sunrise over the river. God knows who or what is needed to deliver the message to a man who's hurting.

When our world is a "sea of uncertainty" as it is today, it's reassuring that we don't have to be afraid of what lies ahead. We can actually get a rush from the unknown because our guide is our Rock. There's nothing unknown to the Great I Am.

4
Burning Daylight

I often wonder why God allowed me to squander 30 years of my life. From the time I became a Christian at age 21 until age 53 my life was lived for self—my needs, my desires, my ways. I lived a life of selfish ambition, no love for people, no compassion, and no interest in what others thought.

My days were consumed with anger, bitterness, lust, jealousy, and greed. Never really knowing what or who I was angry at, I never trusted anyone and always looked out for myself. I felt if I kept people off balance I would have an advantage over them. This warped idea coupled with frequent periods of jealous rage was a prescription for loneliness.

Nobody of any good character wants to be around a person who is a know-it-all, arrogant, boastful, and prideful. As a result I had no friends, no close relationships with people or with God. As Mark Driscoll says, "Bitter people are archeologists; they can dig up the past like it was yesterday."

Even though I had accepted Christ when I was in college, I had failed to follow Him. In his book, *Good to Great in God's Eyes,* Pastor Chip Ingram points out that "when this happens we misrepresent Christ before a watching world."

Today I look back and think, Lord, I could have done so much good if only I had come to know you earlier. Why did you allow me to flounder for so many years? After I was saved I never moved into a relationship with God. At times I would pray and occasionally read my Bible, but the close relationship was never there.

The relationships with my wife and with my son could have been so much better. I would not have burned bridges when I left a job or moved on to another area of life. I would have spent more time helping and giving and spent less time and money on myself.

Paul David Tripp points out that "antisocial attitude is sinful because it causes me to love me more than anything else. We were not designed for selfish, antisocial living; we were designed for the big-sky kingdom of God."

It's strange how God moves His children closer toward Him, sometimes with slow, small steps and occasionally in a downhill rush as the Holy Spirit propels us. When we are stubborn and rebellious, he drags us kicking and screaming, sometimes for years, to a place where he can use us. Pastor Chip Ingram explains, "God develops us in His school of faith."

Today my life is sweet water, the bitterness is mostly gone, and the anger has been replaced by a divine urgency to serve, a promise to obey quickly, and a commitment to live intentionally.

5
Ridge-Runner

The heavy downpour the night before has made the trails muddy and slippery, and the high running streams are an added challenge for the Rugged Faith guys as they roar through the Ozark National Forest on their ATVs. We call this part of the boot camp Ridge-Runner ATV Tours.

Hoops and yells echo across the valley as the multicolored Hondas move in single file up the treacherous ridge road toward the top of Push Mountain. Like little boys released for recess, the men gun the throttles of their machines in anticipation of the morning's adventure.

When you blend power and speed with competition, then season it with an element of danger, you have the perfect recipe for a men's retreat in the wilderness.

As we reach the top of the ridge, we begin to pick up speed and the mud starts to fly. The long train of 4-wheelers begins to snake its way along the old service roads and trails that cut through the rugged hills and hollows of the Leatherwoods.

I love these hills. As a teen, my brothers and I spent many a day hiking, hunting and exploring these roads and trails. And to think 30 years later I have the opportunity to return here and share this country with Christian men who need the beauty and adventure this area offered me as a child.

The sounds, smells, and sights bring back good memories and the hope that these men will remember this day as one of those windows of opportunity that God gives us to enjoy.

The swollen creek from last night's rain has given us an added element of danger. As we approach the first crossing I signal for the guys to shift to low gear and slow down. The swift current could be dangerous to new riders, and the increased depth of the stream can drown out the engines if we hit it too fast.

Having ridden 4-wheelers for several years, I sometimes forget that some of these guys are riding for the first time. I must make sure that I don't lead too fast or assume that everyone is as comfortable on the machines as I am.

Just as each guy is at a different level of experience and ability in the outdoors, each of them is at different places in their walk with the Lord. While it's not always possible to determine another's current status with God, I can usually tell if a guy is nervous or uncomfortable with the speed or with the terrain.

Conquering fear and handling risk produces confidence. As we become more confident in our abilities we begin to enjoy the activity and the fellowship of those around us. It's rewarding to watch as the inexperienced and passive guys begin to grow in confidence and in excitement throughout the day.

God never meant for men to be passive and fearful. It kills our joy and keeps us from reaching our purpose in life. Fear is the number one weapon the enemy uses to keep men passive.

In spiritual matters, God calls us into greater and greater risk because He wants us to trust Him. God's main agenda is for us to trust Him. Think of areas of your life where God wants you to take a risk. Will you trust that He has your back and that He wants the best for you?

Andree Seu of World Magazine says, "Risk taking is nothing fancy, just an everyday pressing into little things that we have no confidence of doing without the help of God."

I compare this to the lack of confidence and the uneasiness that some of these guys feel the first time they come to a stream crossing or to a steep portion of the trail. Once they conqueror these early obstacles, they are ready to take on a larger challenge.

Pressing into little things can be scary. The little things could include starting a new Bible study with your co-workers, inviting your neighbor to a church event, or something as basic as resolving to love the unlovable. Pressing into these little things will daily move us closer to God's will a baby step at a time. After a time of risk-taking in little things God begins to challenge us with larger and larger risks.

The smoothest part of the trail and the part with the best views are along the top of the ridge. It is normally flat on top and the trails are well-worn. We can begin to gather speed after the slow rock crawl to the top of the ridge. With increased speed comes added risk and added reward. Join me today as a Ridge-Runner.

God wants us to move in His shadow, as He moves we move with Him. Sometime it's fast paced; at other times it may be a rock crawl, picking our way over the obstacles of life until He gives us the smoother ridge top.

6
The Tree

As I stared up at the giant white oak, I could picture the monster falling on the corner of the church building.

Pastor Jim, my friend at Three Rivers Biker Church, asked me to cut down and remove a large tree next to the church building.

"No problem, I'll take care of it." I did not realize that it was no ordinary tree. The thing hovered over one end of the church building with a trunk three and one-half feet in diameter and branches the size of my thighs.

Growing up near the national forest we always burned wood to heat our home and I had cut down my share of big trees, but this one scared me because of its proximity to the church.

Three Rivers Biker Church is a new work of God in our community, and the pastor is a close personal friend. God and the Southern Baptist Convention had provided Three Rivers with this new home.

For me to accidentally fell a large oak onto the corner of this gracious gift would be a disaster. For many years the old building had been lovingly cared for by a small congregation of elderly saints. To smash that special place with one of its guardian oaks would be an insult beyond words.

After much study and with considerable doubt, I began to cut the tree. The first thing to do to fell a large tree is to determine the projected angle of descent based on the direction the tree is leaning.

Next I cut a V-shaped notch at the base of the tree in the direction I wanted it to fall. If the notch is properly cut, I can direct the tree to fall in a direction opposed to its natural lean. If the notch is not cut properly, the tree will fall the way it is naturally leaning, in this case toward the church.

The V-shaped notch should be cut about one-third the diameter of the tree which will cause the tree to fall in that direction. Next I began to cut at a slight angle, from the opposite side, into that notch. After I finished notching the tree, I was not at all sure it was going to work.

Just as I was about to make my final cut, out of the corner of my eye, I saw a young man. With my attention directed on the tree, plus the noise of the saw, I had failed to notice his old pick-up truck slip into the parking lot behind me.

He was a shabbily dressed guy with a scruffy beard and unkempt curly hair. He had a slight smile on his face and a twinkle in his eyes. "Do you need any help?" he asked.

"Have you ever cut any large trees?" was my answer.

"Yes, I worked for Graves Tree Service for a couple of years. Do you have a sharp saw?"

I nodded as he took the saw.

After walking around the tree a couple of times intensely studying my work, he skillfully reshaped the V-notch. When that was complete, he took one more glance up the height of the tree, checked the building, sighted his line of fall, and confidently said, "It'll be all right."

As if the saw were a part of his hands, the stranger skillfully sliced through the giant oak, placing it perfectly right next to the little church.

While I stood in amazement, thankful that it had missed the building, the young man was into his old truck and gone, flying down the highway, before I could get his name or say thank you.

What happened? Did God just send me a helper to keep me from damaging this beautiful little church? I had been praying intently for God's help on this tree. Maybe the guy happened to be driving down a narrow country road at just the right moment? I don't think so, but either way, I was relieved and thankful.

In the past I had never believed in guardian angels, but this "Tree Angel" may have changed my mind. God works in mysterious ways, and He uses people to build our faith and to increase our dependency on Him.

7
The Path

The narrow opening in a thick stand of loblolly pines was clearly visible as we topped the rocky ridge. The overnight thunderstorm had moved on and left a dense blanket of fog that was just now beginning to lift.

The forest floor was soft and quiet underfoot. We followed in single-file as Glenn set a brisk pace. Everyone was pumped, and I hardly noticed the 40-pound backpack filled with more than I actually needed for a 2-day hike.

Our party of six early risers had left the truck before dawn and had made good time covering the two miles uphill from the trail-head parking lot to the window in the pines.

We were up at 5:00 a.m. drinking cups of steaming cowboy coffee to wash down Brenda's famous blueberry muffins, and we were off. No burnin' daylight for this crew. Everyone was eager to hit the trail.

After days of planning and preparation it was time to test the legs and lungs on one of the most challenging hikes of my life.

We were here to hike a 26-mile section of the Ozark Highland Trail in Northern Arkansas. This is a stretch of angry thickets and unforgiving Leatherwood wilderness that demands endurance. Leaving the trailhead at daylight would just about put us at the midway point by late afternoon, if all went well.

The trail was clearly marked as we entered the opening in the trees. The well-worn and straight path was a welcome sight after the steep climb we had just finished. In the early light and lifting fog, we're thankful for those who had gone before us to mark and clear the path.

Many times the trail is not so well marked and certainly not straight nor as well-worn. Sometimes it's nearly impossible to tell which way the main trail leads. It's at those times you're thankful to be following an experienced guide like Glenn.

The Book of Proverbs has plenty to say about the path. It describes two possible paths: a path that leads to life and a path that leads to death.

Proverbs 3:5-7 are some of my favorite verses in the entire Bible. They say, "Trust in the Lord with all your heart and do not lean on your own understanding. In all your ways acknowledge Him and He will make your paths straight."

Jesus says, "Trust Me, I won't lead you astray. Others my try to trick and deceive you, but I never will."

He goes on to say in Proverbs 4:18, "The path of the righteous is like the light of dawn." Never hidden in darkness, never covered with fog, when we acknowledge Him as our guide, He will light the way to a path that leads to life.

Proverbs also has a lot to say about a path that leads to death. Proverbs 16:25 warns us that "there is a way which seems right to a man but its end is the way of death."

Proverbs gives many warnings to men who would follow after their own understanding and the wisdom of this world, warnings to avoid being led astray by the sins of lust and greed that seek to entice and entangle.

The day ends with a combination of exhaustion and exhilaration. The first 16 miles of the trail was rough and steep, but with the Pathfinder as our guide we can rest peacefully.

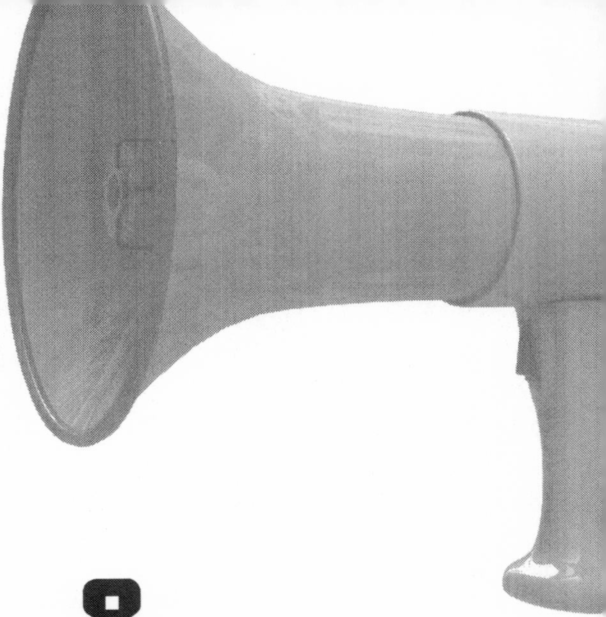

8
A Loud Life

Pastor Francis Chan of Cornerstone Church in Simi Valley, California is an unusual fellow. His book *Crazy Love* is a huge best seller and his second book *The Forgotten God* is also very popular. I enjoy his written words because they read like he speaks; writers call this a writer's "voice."

Chan is a countercultural guy. As the pastor of a megachurch, he accepts a meager salary and lives simply. He gave all the royalties from *Crazy Love* to an organization that works to stop the child sex trade in Asia. In the California material world, this makes him unusual.

One message I got from Chan is that our lives are "too loud." Christians fail to have any spiritual power in their lives because they are too busy to stop and hear what God is saying to them. They let the noise of the world overpower the small, still voice of Almighty God.

The myth of multitasking says that we can do several things at the same time and do all of them well. I tend to think this is not true. I know it is not true for me. I must focus on one thing at a time if I want to do it well. I cannot safely drive and talk on the cell phone. I cannot read and watch TV at the same time if I expect to absorb and retain what I'm reading or enjoy the TV program.

I realize this is also countercultural, but I think the concept of multitasking is a myth. When it comes to time alone with God, I know that it is. Time alone with God requires our total concentration and devotion; if we are to develop an intimate relationship with God, we must give Him our undivided attention.

Whenever we allow constant interruptions to distract us from a special time with God, then our lives become too loud. E-mail, cell phones, TV, and other time-savers can keep us from quieting our minds and our hearts so we can know God and ponder the awesome fact that we are "known" by Him.

One reason that I enjoy the outdoors is because it is an escape from the modern world. To be alone in the wilderness can be a worshipful experience. The glory of God is more evident in nature's cathedral. Isaiah 6:3 says, "The whole earth is full of His glory."

Pastor Paul David Tripp points out that, "The glory of God is in every element of creation. God's glory can be seen in shapes, texture, light, colors, and movements of nature."

If your life is too loud to hear what God is saying, I suggest you spend some time alone in the glorious outdoors and let its sounds, smells, and sights wash away the noise of this world.

9
Make a Way

Much of my life has been a study of the game. For 15 years I was a high school basketball coach. During most of those years my life was controlled by Xs and Os. I spent the majority of my time watching, studying, and thinking about how to win a game.

Maybe those years were not a total waste of time because the following story came to me when I was going through a time of doubt and uncertainty.

In the early days of Rugged Faith I was really struggling with negative thoughts like, "You are not smart enough to lead this ministry, and you are too old to direct an outdoor adventure ministry."

During that time of discouragement, God gave me a message

from my past. Ken Jones was a big offensive guard at Arkansas State University back in the 70s when I was there. Ken was about 6'6" and 250 pounds, and he was fast for a big guy.

During a time of self pity and prayer, God gave me a picture of Big Ken pulling up from the line of scrimmage and leading the sweep around the right side, this picture was in high definition, as clear as a big screen plasma TV.

I could see Ken knocking people down, and right behind him was our little halfback, Leroy Harris. Leroy was about 5'6" and 175 pounds, and had been well coached to stay behind his blocker. He knew if he got out from behind Ken, those big, mean, linebackers would try to kill him.

Staying behind Ken, waiting for an opening, Leroy followed his blocker. Ken wiped out a defensive end and the oncoming safety, and then BOOM the hole opened and Leroy was gone, 70 yards for a touchdown.

This vivid scene had to come from Almighty God. I had not thought of Ken Jones or Leroy Harris for more than 30 years, yet there they were, as clear as if it were today.

God seemed to be saying, "Get behind me, follow me, I will make a way. I don't care how old you are or how smart you are, just stay in my path and I will make a way."

I could see His angels sweeping down across the universe to clear the path, to open a hole, to move obstacles, to allow a little weakling like me to carry God's word to the 68 million American men who do not attend church.

At that moment I surrendered this ministry to God. I said, "Lord, this is your ministry, I will follow your lead. Use me however you see fit."

I continue to call on this picture from the past to inspire and motivate me whenever I start to doubt or get discouraged. Our God is an awesome God. If you will make yourself available He will use you mightily, He will make a way.

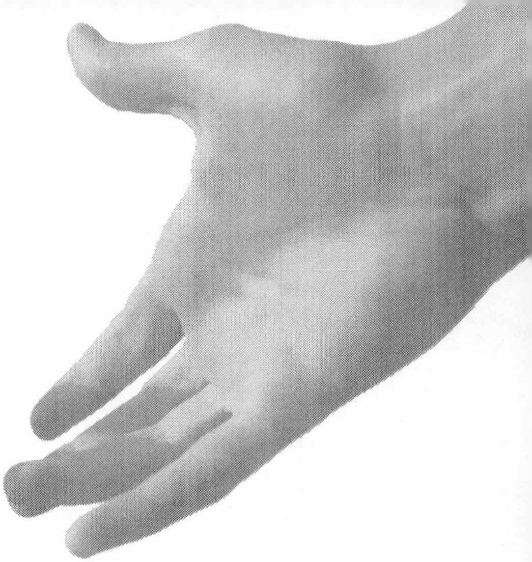

10
The Favorable Hand

Protects Me

Gives Me Blessings

Provides Me Comfort

Keeps Me Humble

Makes Me Grateful

Convicts Me of My Sin

Gives Me Guidance

Directs Me around Obstacles

Disciplines Me Gently

Holds Me Loosely

Pushes Me toward My Purpose

Lifted Me Out of the Pit

Saved Me from Eternal Death

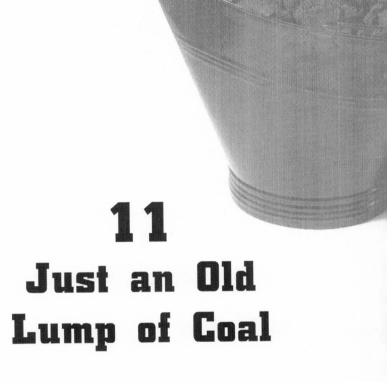

11
Just an Old Lump of Coal

Zechariah 7:11-13 says, "They have refused to pay attention and have turned a stubborn shoulder to God and have plugged up their ears from hearing Him. They made their hearts like flint."

Just as in Zechariah's day, many men have turned a stubborn shoulder to God's message; they have refused to pay attend to anything of God.

I know from experience that a heart of stone is difficult to break through. At one time my ears were plugged and my heart was hard to the things of God. I would tune out anyone who tried to tell me about Jesus and stubbornly resist any constructive criticism of my sinful lifestyle.

Only when other men took an interest in my spiritual life did I begin to respond. Sometimes it takes another rock to penetrate a heart of stone. Sometimes only another man who has been through similar life experiences can reach a man who refuses to hear God's call.

Proverbs 27:17 is a familiar verse. It says, "As iron sharpens iron, so one man sharpens another." It may take time for stubborn, rebellious men to come to God. The hard-hearted man may resist, sparks may fly when iron begins to sharpen iron, and flint can explode whenever it is placed in the fire.

But if we stand firm with steely resolve, God can use us to reach the hard, black heart of the rebellious man. We were all in that place at one time. We have all sinned and fallen short of the glory of God.

As our love and patience works to soften the heart of flint, men can become shining examples of the transforming power of Almighty God. Hebrews 3:7-8 says, "Do not harden your heart." The country songs says, "I'm just an old lump of coal, but I'll be a diamond someday."

12
Fifty-Six

As I write this, I am fifty-six years of age. When I look back on my life I am not at all pleased with what I have accomplished. I have regrets over how I have treated my wife, my son, and my friends. I think of the numerous missed opportunities to do good, to help others, and to serve God. I regret the bridges I have burned, bad things I have done, and time I have wasted on selfish pursuits.

I love my family, but I have loved myself more. For most of my fifty-six years I have lived for self. What I wanted, what I needed, where I wanted to go, what I wanted to do.

This year I came to a shocking conclusion: I am not going to live forever. In fact, I probably won't live more than 20 to 25 years at most. I'm sure that to most people of average and above intelligence this eye-opener comes sooner, but this suppressed bolt of lightning struck me at fifty-six.

Fifty-Six is on Highway 14 just 12 miles east of Big Flat. A couple of gas stations, a country store, and a diner are all that's left of this Mayberry-like town that once had its own high school, post office, and U.S. Forest Service Ranger Station.

As a teen, I remember selling green pine cones to the ranger station for $6 per bushel when the Forest Service bought seed from private landowners. I'm sure they did know that I was cutting down big mature pine trees on government land to harvest the live cones I was selling.

Fifty-Six is also home to Blanchard Springs Caverns, one of the most beautiful caves in the world. I worked summers as a tour guide at Blanchard during the late 70s. The Forest Service hires college students and school teachers as guides during the busy tourist season.

My dad lived and worked in and around Fifty-Six during the Great Depression. As a member of the Civilian Conservation Corps, he helped build roads, bridges, and even the old gymnasium at Fifty-Six.

So, you see, I have a little history at fifty-six, the place and the time. A historic town and a moment in history, fifty-six has some special meaning in my life. As I have gotten older and sometimes wiser, I yearn to live the rest of my life in a manner that is pleasing to God and leave a legacy that my son will be proud of.

From the sale of stolen pine cones to a rebellious tour guide, the list of my fifty-six years of screw-ups would reach to the bottom of

Blanchard Springs Caverns.

But time moves on, and God is a God of grace and healing, so I commit my remaining years to the glory of God. I pledge to spend my days in service to the one who invented time and the only one who knows how much time I have left on this earth.

Psalm 90:12 says, "So, teach us to number our days that we may present to you a heart of wisdom."

This year my goal is to record fifty-six important events that happen in my spiritual life, one for each year I have lived. My plan is to document things like key discoveries in scripture, biblical principles I better understand, and new insights about people.

As I walk closer to the Lord, I expect to build new relationships with people, see regular answers to prayer, experience more joy and peace, and break down sinful strongholds which have dogged me for years.

Fifty-six may sound like a lot of discoveries, but I am on a mission from God, a mission to know Him better and to use my time wisely. I pray that He will make me more productive and allow me to complete some projects I started, to grow the ministry of Rugged Faith, and to encourage others to invest their time wisely.

At the end of year fifty-six I expect to see how God has worked in and through me. Who knows, I may drive over to Fifty-Six and nail my list to the door of the old church house.

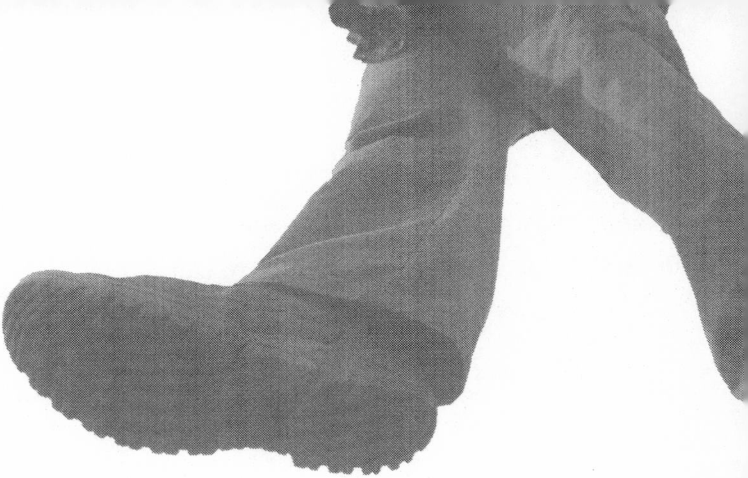

13
Going to the Edge

Rugged Faith strives to take men to the edge, to put them into outdoor situations that offer an element of danger and into spiritual encounters that bring them closer to God.

By blending outdoor adventure and sound biblical teaching on issues that are important, we hope men will find meaning and purpose in their Christian lives.

In an effort to have fuller, richer lives, men have tried to pack too much activity into their schedules. The result is an overflow that has taken many men to the edge of disaster.

John Eldredge, in his book *Wild at Heart,* points out that something special happens whenever men are placed in a wilderness setting, I think it is because today's men are lacking margin. Just as the written page is more readable when it has an appropriate border, men need space in order to come alive, and they find it in the outdoors.

The outdoors offers men an escape from the stressful pace of life that drains them emotionally, physically, and spiritually. It's in the expanse of God's great outdoors that men are renewed and recharged and can return to their first love, God their Father.

During our weekend boot camps we see men change. Stress and uptight attitudes melt away, and they start to look like the Christian men God meant for them to be. They are kinder, full of laughter, and more open to God's word. If only for a few hours, they discover the pace of grace that allows them to slow down and enjoy fellowship with God and with other men.

Chip Ingram says, "To live on the edge is to live with a close reliance on God." What we do with our God-reliant lives will draw others to get involved because "life on the edge is contagious."

According to a new book entitled *Quickology, a Study of the Pace of Life,* the world's fastest city is Singapore, China. The average time it takes to walk 60 feet is just 10.55 seconds. The fastest U.S. city is New York City, which clocks in at 12.00 seconds to cover the 60 feet.

We live in a fast paced society. Americans talk fast, eat fast, and drive fast. We are working longer and sleeping less. We are irritable and impatient people with no time to smell the roses or to taste God's best for our lives.

The American male works an average of nine full weeks more per year than their European counterparts. A recent Gallop poll showed that only 28 percent of American families with children eat together seven nights a week, a 10 percent drop from 3 years ago.

Why do men feel they must go at such a fast pace of life? Andy Stanley in his study entitled Take it to the Limit says its fear that drives men: fear of a wasted life, fear of falling behind their peers, and fear of a loss of status.

Many men are stretched to their limits. They may be at the edge in family relationships, in their finances, or at work, and may have saved no time for a meaningful relationship with the Lord; men have squeezed God out of their lives and replaced Him with busyness and materialism.

If you are living on the ragged edge, God is calling you back to Himself, drawing you back. He is saying, "Come back from the edge, you have reached your limit, save some time for me."

He wants men to live life at a pace where they can be in close relationship with Him. He made us with limits; He set boundaries for our protection. The body needs a certain amount of sleep and exercise. Our government makes laws and rules for our protection, and the Bible gives us moral boundaries designed for our own good.

Just as a stream or river is best enjoyed and used when it is within its banks, the Christian life must have boundaries, limits, and pace. When the downpours come and the stream picks up speed and begins to overflow its banks, the fun ends and danger begins.

When men live at the edge of their limits, bad things can happen. Their marriages flounder, they get neck deep in their work, and when their spiritual lives are swamped with mindless activity, their peace drifts away like an unmanned raft.

Going to the edge with God as our guide is an adventure, and great things can happen. First of all, He will guard and encourage us. Psalm 3:3 says, "You, O Lord, are a shield about me and the One who lifts my head."

If your pace of life has taken you to the scary edge, Jesus offers some much needed R & R. Proverbs 3:8 says, "He offers refreshment to your bones," and Proverbs 3:8 says, "When you lie down your sleep will be sweet."

Singer/songwriter John Prine captured the essence of the problem in his song *The Speed of the Sound of Loneliness*.

> You come home late, you come home early
> You come on big when you're feelin' small
> You come home straight, you come home curly
> Sometimes you don't come home at all.
> What in the world has come over you?
> What in heaven's name have you done?
> You've broke the speed of the sound of loneliness
> You're out there runnin' just to be on the run.

Are you an edge dweller, "out there runnin' just to be on the run"? If you could change just one thing about your life, what change would result in more quality time for relationships with God and with people?

The engine of a Ford Mustang or a Chevrolet Corvette will redline at about 7000 RPM. Redline refers to the maximum engine speed at which the engine is designed to operate without causing damage to the components of other parts of the engine.

The term redline comes from the red bars that are displayed on the car's tachometer and usually denotes the danger area. Many men today are near their red-line, living at such a fast pace they are in danger of damaging themselves and those around them.

14
Kingdom Minded

Getting other ministries and churches to work with us has been a challenge. Even my own church has been reluctant to partner with Rugged Faith for some reason. Maybe it's their fear of not having complete control, a mild form of turf war, or subtle personal jealousy that creeps in.

Some leaders at my church and at other churches have been downright cold whenever I have invited them to join us at our boot camps or other events. Are they so protective of their flocks that they cannot see that as Christians, we are all a part of the family of God?

In his book titled *IT, How Churches and Leaders can Get It and Keep It,* pastor Craig Groeschel describes a kingdom-minded ministry as one which cares more about what God is doing everywhere than what God is doing in their own ministry.

A kingdom-minded ministry is generous and eager to partner with others to get more done for the glory of God. When we develop a kingdom-minded mentality, it creates unity and a synergy that can be dynamic. It's amazing how much we can get done if we don't care who gets the credit.

What does God think about our petty competition for the saints? I tend to think He would not be pleased when churches fail to work together. A selfish, worldly view of ministry looks more like a business than a ministry.

A kingdom-minded ministry is focused like a laser beam on the will of God and not the ways of the world. This focus will allow the ministry leaders to see opportunities to partner with others for the glory of God.

It's a passion of mine to see people become, as Groeschel says, "unreasonably" excited about Christ. We live in a vanilla church age. Many Christians are not excited about God or about life. They spend their days with a constant low-grade frustration, hours of unproductive boredom, and even a state of mild depression.

How much blame do we as ministry leaders have for this malaise that exists among Christians? In Jeremiah 10:21 the prophet says, "Our shepherds have become stupid and have not sought the Lord, therefore all their flock is scattered."

While we cannot completely blame our church and ministry leaders for our current spiritual condition, they must accept some of the criticism for the condition of the church.

When pastors see their work as a career instead of a calling, the church will be seen as just another institution, with no power to change lives.

15
The Leatherwoods

In his book *Lord Change my Attitude,* Pastor James MacDonald writes about attitudes that lead to "wilderness living." Pastor Doug Munton refers to these attitudes as "living in a spiritual cave." Both paint vivid word pictures of men who wander from God or hide from their God given purpose.

I describe these attitudes as "Life in the Leatherwoods." In the Ozarks, where I live there is an area known as the Leatherwoods. John Quincy Wolf wrote a wonderful book with this title about this area. Rugged hills and dense forest make the Leatherwoods a hard place to live. With few good highways and scarce job opportunities, life in the Leatherwoods is tough.

Many see this area of the Ozarks as a mass of brush thickets, briar patches, and scrub forest that is wild and untamed. To others the clear mountain streams and abundant wildlife make this area a diamond in the rough. It's a land that is a struggle to some but a paradise to others.

Life in the Leatherwoods is an apt description for the existence I see in many men. They wear an attitude that is as tough as leather. They struggle to scratch out a spiritual living in a rugged culture. Many live their entire lives and never find their way out of the wilderness.

Most men know that this attitude is destructive, yet they choose to live in a spiritual wilderness of negative rebellion to God, when just over the next hill is a life that will bring them peace and significance.

Men who will allow God to use them can find a promised land wherever they are. However, those warriors in hiding, those men who reject their calling, may languish in the Leatherwoods all their life.

Recently I made a trip back to my past, to our old home place in the Leatherwoods. The old shack has fallen in and the forest has taken over the hard packed dirt yard where we used to play.

I climbed the steep hill in back of the house, up to the "Roaring Spring" where we used to get our water. As I sat there in the mist of the waterfall a cascade of emotions came gushing back. Memories of the days spent alone in the woods. Unfortunately, the bad memories overflowed the good and I found myself in need of God's healing touch.

I have spent many years holding on to bitterness and hate, blaming my parents for many of my emotional problems and broken relationships. Here in this little corner of the Ozarks, on a hillside in the Leatherwoods, God came to me. A wave of peace and forgiveness washed over me, and I was able to release all those old hurts. My rugged, tough-as-leather heart was made as soft as that feather bed in my grandmother's back room.

16
Flood Gates

For years I have had what I thought to be great ideas for ministry. I even acted on a few of them. There was Christian Business Marketplace, an effort to market Christian business books through direct mail. I developed the logo, chose the titles, and printed a slick eight-page catalog. I assumed that Christian businessmen and women would certainly purchase these books and I would be rich and famous. The idea flopped within a few months.

Effort number two was Christian Publishers Showcase, a great concept that also failed. This scheme was to be a display service for small Christian publishers who needed a presence at national conventions. For a fee I would display their books along with the books of several other publishers. When this one failed to be accepted, I thought, "Another good idea that was ahead of its time."

Then there was Good News Publishers Outlet, a retail bookstore that lasted about a year before it folded.

All of these were worthy efforts at ministry, but they all failed because I was doing them for the wrong motives. I wanted to be seen as a super-Christian who was out there doing the work of the Lord. I was more interested in my image than in helping others, more like the money changers in the temple than a sincere Christian.

I didn't understand why my ideas and yearning to serve in ministry were being held back, dammed up. Surely God was waiting for the right time to release them to the world.

I finally came to realize that God must work in me before He will work through me. God showed me that He did not need my great ideas and creative concepts. He wanted my obedience and to develop my character.

The fall of 2008 was a time of floods, tornados, and ice storms for the Ozarks. The area where I live was hit with a triple whammy of natural disasters. These storms caused millions of dollars in damage and lost income for the many small resorts and other businesses that depend on the lakes and the rivers for their livelihood.

Standing on a ridge overlooking Norfork Dam during the flood, God gave me a picture of His awesome power and a message directed straight to my searching heart. As the flood gates opened and the water was released, God seemed to be telling me, "I don't care how many good ideas for ministry you have. I don't need them. I need you to get your heart right, and then I will use you."

As the waters roared over the dam, covering the defenseless

campground and homes in its path, I came to realize that once I get the relationship right, God will open the flood gates, and my ideas, my energy, and my love for Him will overflow to those around me and the ministry will flourish, not because of my efforts, but because He is in it.

Oswald Chambers once said, "The main thing about Christianity is not the work we do, but the relationship we maintain, and the atmosphere produced by that relationship."

17
Stand By

As they gathered at the river, the morning fog was beginning to lift. The cold, crisp April air had a bite of winter to it. The men slowly formed a single-file line along the bank of the Norfork. With collars turned up and hands in pockets, they reverently bowed as I led in prayer.

These times of prayer and Bible reading have become a morning routine at our Rugged Faith Boot Camps. The guys love meeting God here by the river to begin their day.

Today I read from Exodus 14:13, "Do not fear, stand by, and see the salvation of the Lord." This is in reference to the scared and discouraged Israelites whom Moses had led out of slavery in Egypt and was now trapped at the edge of the Red Sea.

With Pharaoh's army behind and the Red Sea in front, the people were mad at Moses for bringing them into the wilderness to die. With the chariots closing in and their faith dwindling, it seemed hopeless.

From my position at the front of the line, my eyes went down the row of men before me. I am always impressed by the quality of the men who come to these events and in awe of what God is doing in the lives of men in this country. I also wonder how many of these men who are here today feel scared, discouraged, or trapped. Out of the forty men who are at this April event, I'm sure some have come in search of deliverance from the bondage of some sin.

These are uncertain times in which we live. Many men feel trapped in unhappy marriages, by oceans of debt, and in dead-end jobs. Like the people of Israel, they may have started out boldly, but over time they have taken their eyes off Jesus and now feel like giving up.

Part of our goal at Rugged Faith is to encourage men to stand firm in their faith. At times it may seem like life is charging at you like Pharaoh's chariots and you want to turn and run. Exodus 14:14 says, "The Lord will fight for you while you keep silent." If you will trust Him, stand by and watch what the Lord will accomplish for you today.

I want to encourage you to hang tough, to stand firm.

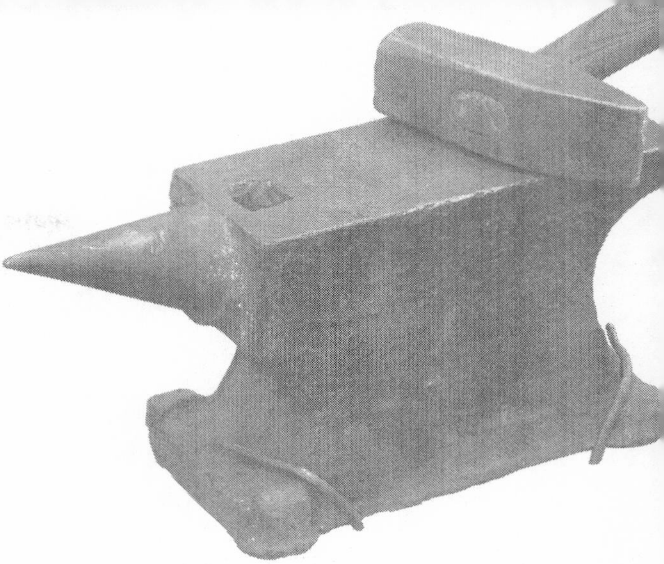

18
Get Real

In his book *Revolution, Finding a Vibrant Faith Beyond the Walls of the Sanctuary,* George Barna makes this important point concerning his research: "We spent several years searching for evidence that God was at work changing lives through churches and discovering how that process worked. While we certainly found some wonderful examples, I was stunned and deeply disappointed at how relatively rare such instances were.

"But our conversations with churchgoing people and congregational leaders led us to the primary source of such transformation; ministries operating outside of the local church. These were not all "Para church" ministries, per se, but were God-centered endeavors taking place outside of a congregational connection.

"These spiritual mini-movements are good evidence that not all legitimate spiritual activity must flow through the local church. Some of these mini-movements include homeschoolers, house churches, biblical worldview groups, various marketplace ministries, and several spiritual disciplines networks."

This rather lengthy quote gives me hope that Rugged Faith can be one of those mini-movements of God that creates opportunities for the Holy Spirit to transform the lives of men.

Barna goes on to point out that today's men, especially those under forty years of age, are looking for encounters with God that are "real, adventuresome, and memorable." I believe outdoor adventure ministries like Rugged Faith can offer all three of these to men.

Our prayer is that we provide leadership that is sincere and authentic, activities that offer an element of danger, stories of faith that are relevant, and that we create lasting memories and offer time alone with God.

A "revolution of meaning" is coming. Men are sick and tired of irrelevant church meetings that honor man more than their Maker. If our churches cannot satisfy this hunger for purpose, men will find it outside the church.

Men are not interested in building and growing institutions and programs. Control leads men to be compliant and to stagnate. Control leads men to become disengaged and bored and to drop out. Let's get real about Jesus and stop playing games.

19

Four Levels of Living

Men are story tellers, so I want to tell you four stories, stories with a purpose, hopefully with a message you can take home with you.

These four stories are based on the Four Levels of Living by David Foster, in his book *No Mediocre Life*. Level one is SURVIVAL, level two is SAFETY, level three is SUCCESS, and level four is SIGNIFICANCE.

We will begin with a survival story. A large portion of my childhood and teen years were spent in the National Forest of the Ozark Mountains, in an area known as the Leatherwoods.

The Leatherwoods are a rugged area with dense forest, steep

hills, and scrub brush; it is a difficult place to hunt and a difficult place for poor families to survive.

There is a great book by John Quincy Wolf called *Life in the Leatherwoods*. The Wolf House is one of the oldest houses in the Ozarks and is located here at Norfork, Arkansas.

My four brothers and I spent countless days roaming through the hills and hollows, hunting, and exploring. Hunting for us was an adventure and a necessity. If we wanted meat to eat it meant we had to kill it. No supermarket hamburger, pork chops, or steak in those days. Our meat was wild game. I have eaten most every kind of wild game native to the Ozarks: deer, rabbit, squirrel, raccoon, plus a few others.

Hunting was an adventure. I remember spending hours alone with only my .22 rifle or my dad's old shotgun, hunting for game or scouting to see what was over the next ridge.

The woods were a safe place for me, an escape from the crowded little house our large family lived in and from the anger and verbal abuse of an alcoholic father.

The kill was important for food, but the hunt itself was the adventure. Tracking rabbits in a newly fallen show or stalking a white-tail deer around the edge of an old field in the late afternoon gave me more pleasure than the actual kill.

I prided myself in my woodsmanship skills that I learned from my dad and my older brothers. My dad was a great hunter, a WWII vet who spent four years fighting the Japanese in the South Pacific. He fought at the Battle of Guadalcanal.

As I get older and look back on those days spent in the woods, I wonder how I ever survived. Since I have become a Christian I can see Gods hand of protection upon me during those years, and I'm more aware and thankful for His love and protection, for the way He kept me in His hand.

The reason I tell this story is because I think many men today live in spiritual survival mode. They live a dull existence in the Leatherwoods of life, just getting by. They struggle to scratch out a spiritual living, hiding from God, never knowing Him fully, never reaching their potential or living out God's plan for their lives.

That's not the way God meant for it to be. He came that we might have life, and have it more abundantly. There's more to life than just survival living

Level two living is safety. There is nothing wrong with living safely, using caution, and being sure before you act. But I think you would agree that its risk that produces character. Without risk or danger, the great expeditions in history would never have been undertaken. Think about the Lewis and Clark 1804 expedition or John Wesley Powell's trip down through the Grand Canyon. These guys did not live safely; they took risk.

Most men are not afraid of risk when it comes to exploration or adventure, but many men spend their spiritual lives in the safety of the upper deck or on the sidelines far away from the action.

They talk about God and watch from a distance, but are afraid to move up closer to the game. They let fear keep them in the cheap seats.

Maybe they think they are not worthy, or don't have the knowledge to move closer to the action. So they play it safe, fail to get involved, let others take the lead in spiritual matters even when God has given them a special problem they were custom-made to solve.

These men are not wimps. They may be rugged and tough in the workplace and with their friends, but when it comes to church or spiritual matters, some might refer to them as "evanjellyfish," evangelicals/Christians with no spiritual backbone, not fulfilling their God-given purpose, living life on safety.

But if we allow Him to, God will call us into greater and greater risk, because He wants us to trust Him.

John Eldredge says, "God did not come to tame men, but to set them free." Guys, your lives are more than a dash between two numbers. Life is not meaningless; it is very purposeful.

In his book *Wild at Heart,* John Eldredge also says many of us live behind a mask, posing as something we are not, protecting ourselves from any chance of being hurt or taken advantage of, living shallow relationships, never letting people get too close, even those who love us, we keep them at a distance.

I love the new song by Brad Paisley called "When I get to where I'm goin'." One of the lines says, "I'll leave my heart wide open, I'll love and have no fears." That's a great picture of how life should be lived.

In the last few months, God has made me realize that He wants me to go deep with people, to love larger, to care more.

Level three living is Success. Many Christians are stuck at level three on the elevator of living. But God has placed us here for a purpose greater than making money and collecting toys. I want to tell you about two recent experiences that contrast worldly success and Biblical success.

Back in January we had a warm Saturday afternoon, and I had the opportunity to float Crooked Creek with three guys from our church. Nothing really eventful happened. We got to ride 4-wheelers, kayak a section of the creek, and fish a little...well, I did tip over and get wet. But the reason I mention this is the nature of the conversation (for once I kept my mouth shut and listened). It was calm, measured, gossip-free talk of things that matter, eternal things, spiritual matters of the heart, compassion for others, concerns for the hurting, needs of our church family.

These are all very successful guys who are at the top of their fields, guys who are living with joy, peace, and balance, guys who are living more than a successful life.

The very next day I had the opportunity to go to Colorado snow skiing with three other guys. I love to ski, and we had planned this trip for several weeks. The snow was fantastic and the weather was great, but what struck me was the difference in the conversations with these three men compared to the three Christian men I had been with the day before.

Again all three of these men are very successful businessmen, well respected in their communities, good guys all. But the two worlds were like night and day; it was the difference between light and darkness.

During this ski trip the talk was of money, things, places, women, problems, more women, and more problems; temporal, short-term matters, nothing of the heart, no concern for the eternal.

Living a successful life in God's eyes is much different than the world's view of success.

You may be a "successful" Christian, teach Sunday school, you might be a deacon, be a good father, read your Bible, and be ethical in business dealings. And that is great; God will honor that.

But there is more...let's allow God to take us to the next level of living, up into the high country, above the tree-line of safety, beyond the comfort of successful living.

Let's step up to another level of living that few men ever reach. When we step up to a life of SIGNIFICANCE, it's like going from class one whitewater rapids to class five rapids. Class one is the bunny slopes, the training wheels of kayaking, kind of like the Norfork or the White Rivers. Class five is for the big boys, the large, complex, gushing, turbulent, waters. We move from a comfortable life of safety and success to a life filled with adventure, danger, and fulfillment.

I'm certainly not the poster boy for living with purpose and significance...for most of my life I have lived an accident-driven life, not a purpose-driven life.

But through prayer and studying God's promises, I have learned that God wants us to live a life of significance, a life of meaning, a life of purpose, and to have joy, love, and peace in our lives. John 10:10 says, "I have come that you may have life, and have it abundantly."

This final story is a familiar story. Gideon's first encounter with God finds this future war hero "threshing wheat in the wine vat in order to hide from the Midianites" (Judges 6:11). Why was this warrior in hiding? He was afraid the Midianites might steal his crop or kill him. He was down in a wine vat to avoid attention.

You know the story. God led Gideon from survival living, out of the wine vat of safety, through success in battle to a life of significance. He built a rugged faith in Gideon that allowed him to defeat an army of 135,000 Midianites with a force of only 3,000 men and free a nation.

God called Gideon into greater and greater risk because he wanted Gideon to trust Him. God used one man to free a nation.

The story of Gideon is a good picture of many men today. Like Gideon, some of God's greatest potential leaders are what Pastor Doug Mutton calls "heroes... in hiding."

God knows your fears just as He knew the fears of Gideon. God sees in you what others may not. He looked at Gideon and saw a great warrior and leader; He looks at you and sees great potential. Gideon took a risk by trusting God, and God raised him up to a life of significance.

George Barna Research shows that the number one fear of most men is living a wasted life. Men want to matter, to make a difference, to leave a positive legacy.

Chuck Swindoll says "We aren't just thrown on this earth like dice tossed across a table. We are lovingly placed here for a purpose."

Pastor Bill Hybels points outs that "God has custom-designed you with your unique combination of personality, temperament, talents, and background to accomplish His purposes."

In his book *12 Ordinary Men,* John MacArthur points out that the men Jesus called were perfectly average. He knew their faults long before He called them. The twelve were not from the religious establishment; their call was not based on education, pedigree, or experience.

Some were big, proud, boastful loud-mouths, like Peter. Others were the strong silent type like Andrew. They were ordinary men.

Many of the "good to great" leaders profiled in Jim Collins's book are shy, unimposing, humble guys. So don't sell yourself too short by not expecting God to work in and through your life.

He might call you to accomplish far more than you ever thought you were capable of, not for your glory, but that the borders of His kingdom might be expanded.

I'll finish up with this illustration. Those of you who have done any carpentry work know that there is a formula to designing and building steps. The three parts of the steps are the stringer, the tread, and the riser.

The stringer is the support pieces that extend from one floor to the next; the tread is the place you walk, and the riser is the lift or step up.

Building rugged faith is much the same; it requires the stringer or support of God's Word. Things like answered prayer give support to our faith, as does seeing God work in our lives and the lives of others.

Building rugged faith also requires the tread, or the daily walk: getting up every day, putting one foot in front of the other, never giving up. But the joy is in the rise, or the step up, but it requires work. The Statue of Liberty has 354 steps to the crown, 22 stories. The climb is a lot of work, but it's worth the effort.

Let me ask you a couple of questions. Is your current level of living worthy of the sacrifices of those who have gone before you:

your parents, your grandparents, the sacrifices made by your Lord and Savior?

Are you satisfied with your current level of living? I don't know about you, but I want more than just survival. I don't want a safe, comfortable faith. Even more than what the church would call a successful faith; I want a rugged faith that honors God and a faith that people will remember when I'm gone, an ever growing faith that risks it all; that steps up to a calling.

I want to encourage you today; don't settle for spiritual survival in the Leatherwoods, climb out of the wine vat of safe living and resist the slippery slopes of worldly success.

With God's help, let's step up to a life of significance.

20
Music of Life

The twang of the steel guitar fills the local VFW building as middle-aged couples shuffle around the concrete dance floor. Smells of stale beer and cigarette smoke hang in the air. Pickup trucks huddle close together in the nearly full parking lot as family, friends and fans stream into the music hall.

On stage is a collection of middle-aged, semi-pro musicians who are here more for the love of their craft than for their meager take. Steel, bass, drums, and lead guitar make up the group. Cowboy hats and boots are the preferred, but not required, attire. The smooth, country voice of the lead singer sets the tone for the night of fun and fellowship.

Lynn made singing look effortless. On stage with an easy smile and a confident manner, he could deliver a Haggard or Ray Price tune to rival the original, but those of us who grew up with him knew that he had spent endless hours refining his sound.

The once shy, backward, country boy had made himself into a professional entertainer through hard work and constant study. His love for music was second only to his love for Michelle and their sons Kevin and Tom.

From as early as I can remember, my brother Lynn loved music. His first guitar was purchased with money earned from picking cotton, and his first song was "Wildwood Flower." After days of agonizing practice we were all thrilled when he finally moved on to song number two.

The eldest of six children, Lynn Ward was born into poverty in 1949 and died in his childhood home of Calico Rock, at the age of sixty. The son of a saintly mother and an alcoholic father, Lynn got the best and the worst from both. He knew Jesus and was well acquainted with Jack Daniels.

In a day when most people love things and barely tolerate one another, Lynn genuinely loved people and lived a simple life. He was most at home with family, friends, and his music.

He often said, "I work so I can play music." He knew and was known far and wide by those in the country music world. As a teen he would walk for miles, carrying his old guitar, for a chance to share his music with one or two other pickers or with a living room full of friends.

As someone who is not the least bit musically inclined and with absolutely no rhythm, I can't fully understand the heart and mind of those like Lynn who absolutely live for music. Music was his life and I'm 100 percent positive he was listening to a country song on the CD player in his old van as he turned into the driveway for the last time.

Other than family, Lynn and I had very little in common, but I miss my brother. I wish I could talk to him one more time and tell him I loved him and hear him get excited about the latest old western swing band he had just heard.

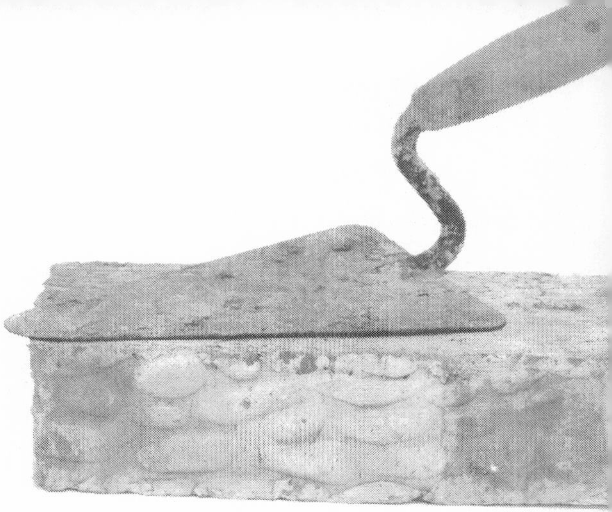

21
Down the Line

Many times I hear people talk about the fact that they grew up in a Christian home. They talk about their grandparents who modeled the faith or great-grandparents who were preachers and who handed down a legacy of following the Lord.

Recently, a friend showed me a Bible that belonged to his great-great-grandmother. It was worn and weathered with the rich patina of constant use. Faded notes from days gone by filled the margins of the yellowing pages. Handwritten prayers from the past were tucked neatly inside the old book.

Like a treasure from Antiques Road Show, he rushed to show me this special gift. I could hear the pride of ownership in his voice.

I wonder if those who come from Christian families realize how sacred the legacy of love is. Do they realize that to be a part of a long line of love is a special blessing?

I realize that God does not have any grandchildren, only sons and daughters. Each one of us must choose to accept Him or reject Him. Our gift of salvation cannot be passed on from one generation to the next.

However, many of us who were not raised in a Christian home and cannot enjoy this legacy are doubly determined to be the start of a family who follows the Lord – to pass on stories, writings, traditions, and examples which our children and grandchildren can look back on as a blessing.

A parent who is more interested in providing the latest toys, gadgets, or designer jeans for his children is missing a window of opportunity to provide something much more meaningful than things.

By leaving a Christian legacy, you are laying the foundation which your offspring can build on. Your work now can pay huge benefits to those who come after you. Cool wears off, but character lasts. A long line of love can stretch for stretch from generation to generation. Don't neglect your part; pass it down the line.

22
The Hunt

As I have gotten older and look back on my days spent in the dark woods of the Ozarks. I wonder how I ever survived on wild game, flour gravy, and powdered milk. What kept me from severe injury or death during some of those longs days and nights when I would plunge headlong into caves, gullies, and creeks in search of game and adventure?

Since I have become a Christian I can see God's hand of protection upon me and my brothers during our youth. I'm more aware and thankful for His protection and for this wondrous creation God has placed us in.

Today I still hunt, but for different reasons and for different game. Hunting has taken on a more urgent tone. It is one of the most exciting things I do. The skills I need have changed from woodsmanship to discipleship. The consequences of this hunt can mean the difference between eternal life and death.

Hunt is the name of this special, life-changing, dangerous adventure. Follow me as we take a closer look at some endangered species, and look at ways we can help them.

Hurting...Wherever we look in this world there are hurting people. At work, at school, at the grocery store, even at church, there is no shortage of hurt and problems to go around. A famous business executive once said, "Problems are my business and business is very good." Most likely the hurt is of the heart, the loss of a loved one, a divorce, a rebellious or runaway teen, or an elderly parent who consumes energy and time. Listening and love are the keys to the hunt for the hurting. No need to say, "I know what you are going through, or I know how you feel," because it won't matter to them while they are in the middle of this mess. I'm no expert on the hurting and I'm new to compassion and mercy (these are not my spiritual gifts), but I am trying to be on the lookout for signs of the hurting.

Unchurched...You want to talk about big game hunting, this is the ultimate. With an estimated 6.5 billion people on the planet and only about 1 million Christians, this unchurched group is big. We don't have to go to Africa to find them; they are our neighbors, our families, and our co-workers. They are lost as geese and searching for meaning and purpose in their lives. We can be a light in the dark woods of this world to guide them to Jesus. Are you refining your skills to hunt for the unsaved? I encourage you to. Every time we help lead an unchurched person to the Lord, we are helping to reduce the size of the other three groups of the hunt: the hurting, the needy, and the troubled.

Needy... I grew up in a very poor family. My father was a WWII vet who was disabled and an alcoholic. He had a fifth grade education and could not hold a job. My four brothers and I grew up as a part of the needy. Food, clothing, and shelter were scarce. I know what it means to be in need. I also know what it is like to have plenty. God has blessed my wife and me with material blessings beyond what I could ever imagine. On our hunt, the needs of the poor should be in our sights. We can help them help themselves, tell them about Jesus, and give to good organizations like Feed the Children and to our local food banks. God will bless those that give a cup of cold water to the needy.

Troubled... If you are looking for trouble, you won't have far to go. Our world is filled with lonely, depressed, guilt filled, worried people. My doctor once said, "I should put Prozac in the city water supply," because so many of his patients were on this anti-depressant medicine.

I don't know if it is the times in which we live or what, but I do know from experience there is a treatment for the troubled because I have been one of them.

The old song says, "There is a Balm in Gilead to make the wounded whole, there is a balm in Gilead to heal the sin-sick soul." The treatment for the troubled is Jesus. He can calm the worried and troubled mind, He can be a friend to the lonely who feel unloved, and He can remove a lifetime of guilt that has kept you crippled. I'm not a psychologist or a trained counselor, but I know trouble when I see it.

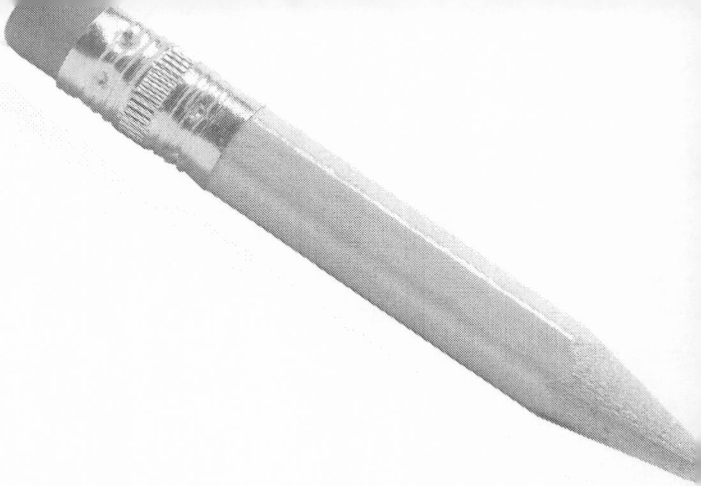

23
I Have Not Forgotten

1. People I have mistreated .... Seek forgiveness
2. Bridges I have burned .... Try to rebuild them
3. Blessing I took for granted ..... Thank God every day
4. Kind acts by strangers .... Pass them on to others
5. Friends who were loyal ..... Tell them you remember
6. Opportunities I have missed ...... Today is a new day
7. The times God protected me ..... Never, never forget
8. Books that have moved me .... Read them again
9. Men of integrity .... Copy them in every way
10. God's promises .... Lean on them every day

24
Freedom

As we celebrate Independence Day I am reminded of the stories my father told of his experiences in the South Pacific during WWII.

Over 300,000 brave American soldiers gave their lives in that war to protect the freedoms you and I have today.

My dad was reluctant to talk much about the war, but occasionally he would tell us about the horrors and adventure he experienced during four years in far off places like the Philippines, New Guinea, and Australia.

I have a newspaper clipping from his hometown paper telling of him being lost in the fierce Battle of Guadalcanal in 1942. He told us of how he hid in a cave for several days, after being separated from his outfit during the bombardment of the island. Living on bugs and bad water until he could find his way back to his outfit, God protected him or I would not be writing this today.

Freedom is hard fought for. During times of war men on both sides fight and die until one side surrenders.

Freedom in Christ comes only "with" surrender. Surrender of our agendas, our wills. When we say, "Lord, I turn it all over to you," a peace comes that allows us to live lives that matter.

As an American on the July 4th, thank a veteran for the freedoms we enjoy as a nation, and as a Christian, thank God that surrender brings a freedom that passes all understanding.

In his book *Man's Search for Meaning* Victor E. Frankl says we need a "Statue of Responsibility" on the west coast to supplant the "Statue of Liberty" on the east coast, that without one the other is only part of the story. With freedom comes responsibility.

Freedom and liberty are gifts from Almighty God to all men and women, but with these gifts come the duty to be responsible.

25
King's Highway

We love to travel, and God has blessed us with many opportunities to visit interesting places here in the U.S. and around the world. We normally drive, or on occasions when we fly, we will rent a car and drive the back roads of the area we are visiting.

America's highways are as varied as the landscape, from eight-lane super freeways that surround our cities to the steep and crooked Road to Hana on the island of Maui in Hawaii. On this 50-mile road you will cross 51 one-lane bridges as it snakes along the coast of the island. We feel that we are better able to see the country and experience the culture whenever we drive the roads.

I love history and recently read that during the 1600-1700s the Spanish priests built a chain of missions up and down the coast of California. This became known as the El Camino Real or the King's Highway.

The Christian life can sometimes be like a journey. It can have many turns and twists. Our King never promised us that life will be a smooth super highway; sometimes the road gets bumpy and full of pot-holes. But if we will trust in His promises and look for His warning signs, the King's Highway will lead us home. I so look forward to that day when my heavenly father will ask, "How was your trip? Welcome home."

26
Gear Your Life

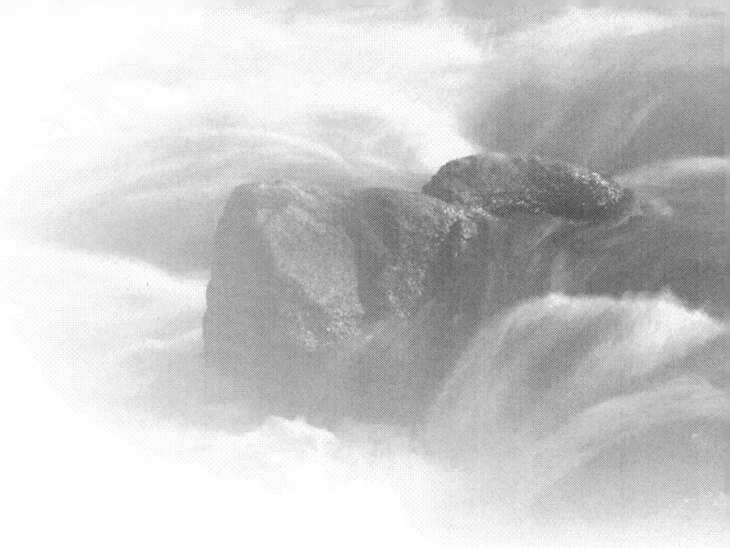

27
River of Life

Brazil is a big, beautiful country with a diverse landscape and numerous natural resources. The people are warm and friendly and the pace of life is slow and easy. Nobody gets in a hurry. You don't need a watch in this country.

The Amazon River dominates much of life in northern Brazil. Many people make their living by fishing so the giant river and its tributaries are the life blood of the region.

The Amazon is the largest river in the world. By volume, it carries more water than the world's next ten largest rivers. It can be up to six miles wide in some places and is over 200 miles wide at its mouth where it empties into the Atlantic Ocean.

Near the city of Manaus in northern Brazil, the Rio Negro, or Black River, merges with the Amazon. The locals call this "the meeting of the waters". The Rio Negro is very dark, almost black in color, and the Amazon is a brown or muddy orange color. For several miles the two rivers run side by side before the massive flow of the Amazon swallows up the black water of the Rio Negro.

The world is moving much like the river. The wide, mass of people flow along, moving in lock step with a culture that rejects God. Those of us who are Christians and fight the flow of the world must paddle hard and rely on the grace of God to keep from being swallowed up by a sinful society.

Picture a clear ribbon of moving water surrounded by a massive, muddy river, flowing around, over, and beneath you. This is the picture of a Christian in the world.

We are in the middle of the culture, moving against the flow, and if we are to remain safe and clean, we must obey His Word, resist the current of the culture, and allow the River of Life to carry us home.

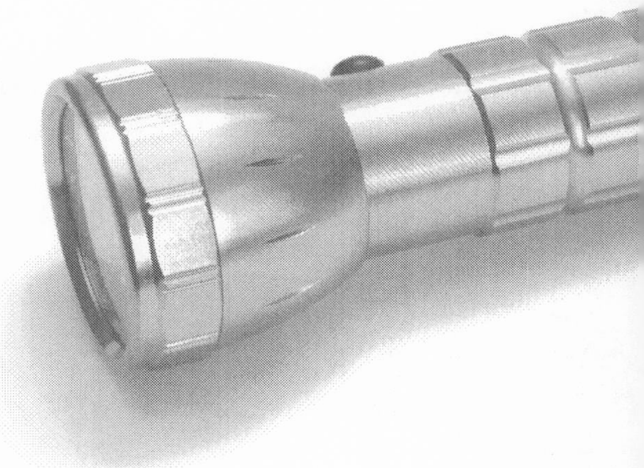

28 Total Darkness

For several years I worked as tour guide at Blanchard Springs Caverns near Mountain View, Arkansas. During the summer I would lead groups through this beautiful underground wonderland that is operated by the U.S. Forest Service.

The two tours available for viewing are the Dripstone Tour and the Discovery Tour. Both require you the walk about a half mile along well lighted paths to view the cave formations.

At some point on the tour the guides would stop the tour and turn out all the lights. This would usually occur at a safe seating area with guard rails.

Inside a cave there is no natural light. Only total darkness exists at 300 feet below the surface. Occasionally the dial of someone's wristwatch could be seen and it seemed to glow like a spotlight in this place where no other light was found.

This was always a good reminder to me that it only takes a little light to illuminate a dark place. This is a discovery that many Christians ignore.

I sometimes use a flashlight with batteries to make this point. The batteries are the power source for the light. It takes all three batteries working together to produce light. I point out that our Christian life is much the same; the three batteries represent prayer, Bible study, and fellowship with other believers. Whenever one of these is missing, we do not shine as brightly in the dark world as God intended.

Jesus calls us to be light in a dark world. Our lives are to show others the way to Christ. Jesus said, "I am the light of the world," and He commands us to shine the light of His love that is living inside us, to be a beacon of hope to a world that is lost in total darkness.

29
When Lightning Strikes

Near Durango in southwestern Colorado is a unique challenge known as "Soaring Tree Top Adventures." Located in a valley along the Animas River, John Roy and Dionne Beggrow have created an absolutely amazing series of zip lines that carry guests between the tops of huge Ponderosa pines.

After a few minutes of instruction which stresses safety, you strap on a climbers harness, climb up to a steel platform that is suspended in the top of a 200 year old tree. Once there the tour guides, known as "Sky Rangers," attach you to a cable suspended between two trees and you're off, zipping to the next platform at speeds that can reach up to 30 miles per hour.

With 22 zip lines in all, "Soaring" is the largest tree top adventures course in the world. These huge pines have been in the valley for years and great care has been taken to protect them.

The Sky Rangers point out trees that have been hit by lightning. Large gashes run almost the full length of some of these 150-foot-tall trees.

They inform us that these trees have a way of healing themselves by going almost dormant in order to divert sap and nutrients to the wounded portion of the tree. After healing the tree can come back stronger than ever.

As Christians, our lives can sometimes be struck by the tragedy of pain, sickness, or the death of loved ones. These trials can leave scars on our hearts that seem to never heal, leaving us bitter, guilt ridden, and broken.

But thankfully God has designed a way to heal the scars, to take away the pain, and make us better than new. He sends a special healing balm of his love and comfort to those who seek Him.

Time and nature heal the damaged pines while the Holy Spirit covers his children with a glory that's brighter and more powerful than Rocky Mountain lightening.

30 Misdirection

Razorback football is a way of life for a lot of us during the fall and winter. The University of Arkansas has a long tradition of excellence in college athletics.

The "Hogs" always seem to have speed and a hard-hitting defense. Their aggressive pass rushes and blitzes sometimes leave the defense vulnerable to misdirection plays by the offense.

Misdirection reminds me of a story a friend of mine tells of a four-year-old daughter who is misbehaving. The father scolds her and says, "She is such a little sinner."

This story makes me think that God must see us that way when we sin. We try to fool Him by acting holy in one area of life while we continue to sin in another.

We use misdirection like the football teams. We say, “Look over there God,” as we attempt to slip our sin past the Creator of the universe. How lame!

“Such a little sinner” is a label Christians need to get past. We should not be baby Christians any more. It’s time to grow up and feed on solid spiritual food of the Word of God.

31
Be an Asset

To Your God .... Use Your Spiritual Gifts

To Your Wife .... Love, Protect, Provide

To Your Kids .... Discipline, Love, Teach

To Your Church .... Join, Give, Lead

To Your Parents .... Support, Honor, Respect

To Your Friends .... Loyalty, Trust, Accountability

To Your Neighbors .... Helper, Example, Witness

To Your Community .... Vote, Volunteer, Build

To Your Country .... Duty, Pride, Service

To Yourself .... Surrender, Pray, Grow

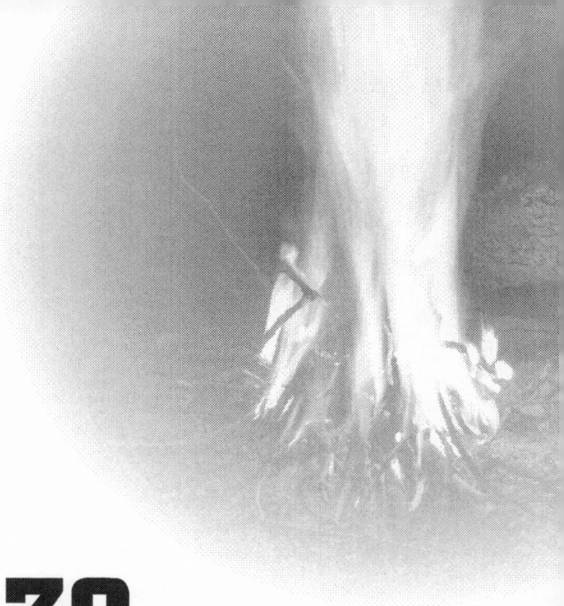

32
Acts of God

Earthquakes .... Cracks in a hard heart

Tornados .... Twisted minds are calmed

Hurricanes .... The eye of the blind is opened

Floods .... A River of Grace to save

Forest Fires .... A burning desire to know Him

Drought .... Living water to the dying

Lightning .... A light in a dark world

Tsunami .... Waves of overwhelming love

Volcanoes .... Able to move mountains

33
Lone Rock

I want take you to a place called Lone Rock. From the name you might picture a standing stone along a rugged coastline or a single giant boulder in the middle of a barren desert.

You would be wrong. Lone Rock is a small community located in the Ozark Mountains of northern Arkansas. Surrounded by tall pines and steep hills, this wide place in the road would be easy to miss if you looked down at your Garmin.

As I drive past the Lone Rock Baptist Church, I picture God calling a man to this remote burg many years ago. God does that, you know. He finds a guy who might not fit in at the big-city mega-church, or a green, young pastor fresh out of seminary, and plants him in one of the thousands of "Lone Rocks" all over this world.

In Mathew 16:18 God says, "I will build my church," and He is doing it. We are His building blocks, each stone carefully chosen and lovingly placed in the walls of the church with Christ as our cornerstone, the foundation, the rock on which the church is built.

Whenever I look across my home church, I marvel at how God has brought together such a diverse group of believers. I live in a small town of 10,000 people, but the mix of gifts and talents in our church come from all over the nation, a marble cake of believers who work together to form one body.

Lone Rock might also describe a lot of men today, living in isolation, trapped in a lone wolf lifestyle, not willing to share themselves or their time for fear of being seen as weak or unmanly.

Men that cannot get out of Lone Rock will never reach the place God has planned for them; they get comfortable in the friendly confines of me, myself, and I, selfishly standing alone, while God yearns for them to be a part of the building blocks of His church.

Push Mountain Road twists and turns through the Ozark National Forest on its way to Lone Rock. This steep, narrow ribbon is a popular route for bikers; it's been the site of numerous crashes and several deaths.

The mix of slow moving log trucks, local ranchers, leaf peepers, and daredevil bikers is a recipe for disaster along this collection of switchbacks.

Our society is laden with danger for men on their way to lone rock. Men must be engaged if they are to make an impact of our culture. God does not bless us so we can be egotistical, arrogant, aloof, or self centered. He blesses us so we can be a blessing to others.

John Wesley said it best that "the Bible knows nothing of solitary religion." Lone Rock might be a nice place to visit, but men can't live there.

34
Vision

As men, we often lead our lives, our businesses, our families, and even our ministries by the wisdom of the world rather than by the wisdom of Almighty God.

By relying upon advice from Amazon's Top Ten business books, falling back on past experience, or just winging it, we run the risk of, as my friend Steve Henderson of Christian Consulting says, "starting big but finishing small."

Proverbs says, "Without vision the people perish." The same is true of a business, a family, or a ministry. If we don't have a clear understanding of where we are going we may never get there. Vision is to begin with the end in mind.

As Christians we should always strive for a godly vision, seeking His advice, His ways, and His plan before we move out in ministry.

As a recovering "marketing minister," I have learned the hard way that my way of doing ministry is not always God's way. There is never a time to be rude, to disrupt unity, or to minister under our own power.

Bible scholar and prophesy expert Jimmy DeYoung points out in his message entitled Steps through Revelation that after the Rapture, those of us who are saved will receive crowns based of our good works, but will experience loss for those works performed under our own power.

Godly vision begins, proceeds, and finishes with one purpose: to see God glorified. Bruce Wilkinson says, "To minister with a godly vision is to attempt something so large that failure is guaranteed unless God shows up."

Larry Page, who is the director of the Arkansas Faith and Ethics Council, recently spoke at our church and his topic was "Godly Vision." His message used the life of Nehemiah as an example of a man working with a godly vision.

Only with much prayer, humility, and seeking of God's face was Nehemiah able to complete the task. The vision was God's vision, not Nehemiah's. He was simply a tool in the hands of the wall builder.

Page made ten crucial points which we must follow if we are to experience godly vision:

1. We must be in right relationship with God through prayer and a humble spirit.
2. We must have a heart for others, including those with

whom we are partnering to complete God's plan.

3. We must survey the problem and seek to understand the scope of the vision.
4. We must be able to explain the problem or the need in order to inspire others to join us.
5. We must be persistent, never giving up, but always looking up to the Father.
6. We must be ready to defend the vision, to overcome resistance from those who would ridicule and attempt to discourage us.
7. We must seek to share the vision with others and ask for their help to carry it out.
8. We must always seek God's favorable hand upon the work we are doing.
9. We must always remember that a godly vision is spawned by faith and is greater than sight.
10. We must always keep in mind that the purpose of the vision is to bring glory to Almighty God.

A godly vision is a road map to success. The wisdom of this world will lead us astray, but those who work God's plan with find fulfillment and ultimate victory.

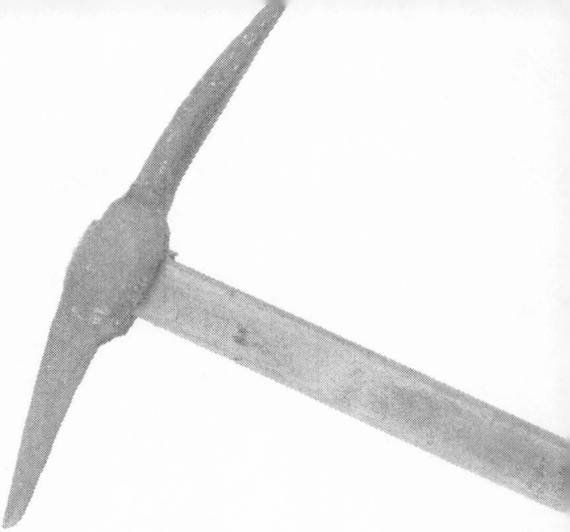

35
Gold

In these tough economic times we have seen gold, silver, and other precious metals sky-rocked in price. Gold has been as highs as $1450 an ounce and silver as high as $30 an ounce. Some of the talking heads on Wall Street say gold may reach $5000 an ounce before it's through.

Men have always tried to find security in wealth. The Forty-Niners braved the heat of desert crossings and deadly winters in the Rockies to make their way to the California Gold Rush of 1849. Again in the 1890s the Klondike gold strike in the Yukon Territory beckoned men to sell everything and set out north in search of gold.

With gold pans, picks, shovels, and slouch boxes, these rugged miners would spend long, backbreaking days in the cold mountain streams and in the dark, dangerous mine shafts, going for the glitter and clawing for the color of gold.

God has a lot to say about money and wealth. He warns us of the dangers of greed and the folly of trusting in material things. Many men spend most of their waking hours in search of the false sense of security and short term pleasure that money offers.

In tough times it's God, not gold, that satisfies. It's when we realize that as we begin to mine nuggets of wisdom from the stream of living water, we will find true wealth.

36
Rescue

The amazing rescue of the miners in Chile can teach us some important lessons about survival, and about the human spirit. It's a story of courage and hope. For those of us who work with men, it's a story of hope. The no-man-left-behind resolve that we saw in the Andes Mountains is what's needed in churches today if we are to build an effective ministry to men.

The whole rescue operation had one single purpose: get every man out safely.

A single-minded approach to planning and execution was employed from the very beginning. Authorities asked the world for help. No national pride or politician's ego stood in the way.

Ideas, experts, and equipment were brought in from around the world. A high tech camera from Japan, special cable from Germany, drills and drilling experts from America, all working together to rescue the 33 men trapped over 2000 feet below the surface of the earth.

As days turned into weeks the trapped miners were sent survival supplies of food, water and medicine. The rescue team contacted NASA for advice on how men deal with long term isolation. A video camera and a phone were sent down through a small shaft. We could see the men and talk with them, yet they were still trapped.

As workers began to drill a larger escape shaft the miners were told it might take months to reach them. Hope seemed to be collapsing. Can you imagine the feelings of loneliness, isolation, and desire those men must have felt?

Greg Hall of Drillers Supply International of Houston, Texas, along with Brandon Fisk of Center Rock Drilling, led the drilling rescue team. The men lived and worked in close quarters during the 33 days of drilling.

Greg said, "We became very tight during those long days. We had a shared purpose of reaching those men who were trapped." The team of twelve drillers and techs were together 24 hours a day for 33 days.

Many experts said the type of curved, twisting shaft required would be impossible to drill. Hall, a deacon in his church, said, "Prayer played a huge role in this job. God drilled this hole; I just had a good seat."

Friends and family members waited above ground at what

became known as Camp Hope. Wives and children cried, worried, and prayed for those entombed a half mile below.

Trapped in a small area the size of a typical living room, 33 men waited to be rescued. On day 69 the 28-inch escape shaft was ready and a capsule was lowered into the mine.

This specially designed human rescue pod was called the "Phoenix." The missile-shaped, steel cage was just barely large enough for a man to stand up in.

One by one, over a 22 hour span, the trapped men were hoisted from darkness and brought into the light.

One of the rescued miners said, "For the past ten weeks I have been between God and the devil. They fought, God won."

The world watched as these mostly unknown men were saved from the depths of a gold mine in the northern Atacama Desert. This is the driest place on earth with less than one inch of rain per year, but on this day tears of joy covered this dry and thirsty land.

Stories of hope, survival, and rescue can touch men's hearts. The lost, the impossible, and the danger can stir men's blood because we can all identify with those who are trapped. Perhaps not physically trapped, but trapped in debt, a bad marriage, a miserable job, or some emotional prison. Men respond to stories of rescue.

Whether in the barren Andes Mountains of Chile or on the busy streets of Chicago, or Chillicothe this should be our mission as Christians: to rescue men who are in darkness, men who may feel as if they have very little hope of being saved, men who are buried in guilt and trapped deep in their sin.

As Christians, this is what God calls us to do. To rescue the lost, help the hurting, and save the dying. We must deliver the light of the Gospel to men in darkness and remind them there is hope in Jesus Christ.

If you're willing, God will use you right here in your hometown to reach men who are trapped. Your church can be Camp Hope to men in your community who have all but given up and see no way out.

Our mission is the man. Our goal is no man left behind.

Key points thast we can take from this story:

1. A single-minded purpose of seeing men brought to Jesus.
2. The realization the all men are important to God and no man should be left behind.
3. Form a team of men who will do whatever it takes to reach the men of their church and their community. There is no "Plan B"; you are the only hope for the men in your community.
4. Learn from others. Don't try to reinvent the wheel.
5. Put aside pride, ego, and the need for individual recognition. Give God all the glory. It's amazing what we can accomplish when we don't care who gets the credit.
6. Be creative (develop the rescue pod) in your planning and persistent in your mission, always seeking God's will through prayer.
7. Make your church "Camp Hope," a place where men can be rescued from darkness.

37
Partner

A very successful businessman once told me, "Never get involved in a partnership, it's the quickest way I know to turn good friends and loving family members into your mortal enemies."

And the sad truth is most partnerships do fail. Even the ultimate partnership, marriage, fails over 50 percent of the time.

Every year millions of marriage and business partners call it quits. Not just because of financial reasons, though it is the most common reason, but because of the inability of the partners to agree on which direction the partnership should go, and hundreds of other less crucial issues facing the pair.

After reading this, you may be asking yourself, "If we can't make human partnerships work, how on earth can we possibly partner with God?"

When I say we can partner with God, I don't mean to imply that you are, or ever will be on equal with God. I am simply saying that God will use you to accomplish His work here on earth if you make yourself available.

If you could choose anyone in the world to be your partner, who would it be? I'm not talking about a marriage partner (drop the fantasies), I'm talking about a business partner. Who would you choose? Bill Gates, Warren Buffet, Steve Jobs? All great businessmen, all very successful, but even these guys aren't perfect.

After everything I have heard about and experienced in partnerships, I want a partner who is perfect, who knows it all, owns it all, sees the future, places and replaces world leaders, even controls the wind and the waves.

In most partnerships, one partner will have gifts where the other has gaps and vice versa. One partner may be great with accounting and numbers, while the other may be a great salesman, or good in customer service. With God as your partner, only one partner has gaps in ability, in knowledge, or in resources, and guess what, it "ain't" God.

In his new book, *You Were Born for This,* Bruce Wilkinson points out that, as Christians we can "partner with God to deliver special miracles from heaven everyday of your life."

To partner with the creator of the universe is an option we cannot afford to pass up. Don't miss the best decision you will ever make.

Wilkinson goes on to say, "you may feel that you are completely unprepared and unqualified to partner with God." I think this would apply to many of us who see God on a level that does not require our meager talents to fulfill His purpose. But that's not true; God yearns for our involvement in His plans. He molds, tests, and prepares us until we are ready and willing to join Him.

Yes, with God as the senior partner, a lifetime of service, purpose, and fulfillment is possible. When you surrender to the perfect partner, your marriage, your family, and your life will be on the fast track to significance.

38
Time

We all try to hold onto that vapor we call life. It's oh so quick, moving from twenty-something to retirement in an instant. Gone before we know it, we are so busy living, we miss life.

When we realize how fleeting it really is, it's too late. At fifty-five I looked up one day and it was gone. Friends, family, career had all passed me by and I had missed the best of them all.

A life is a terrible thing to waste. We come into this life with so much God-given potential and promise, and most of us fail to recognize it until it's too late.

Why does wisdom come so late in life? Why doesn't God give us wisdom at twenty-five instead of at fifty-five? Why can't the keen eyes of seventeen see what the failing vision of seventy-five sees?

Experience is the best teacher, yes, but why didn't God create all of us with the experiences of those who came before us so we aren't at middle age or older when we understand there's more to life than money, power, and sex?

Maybe I'm a slow learner, but impact and purpose never occurred to me until I was past my prime. Water under the bridge, bridges I had burned, bridges I had been too fearful to cross, can all be seen clearly from the far bank of middle age.

I am motivated and inspired by the passage from Job 42:12 that says, "Job was blessed by God greater in his latter years than in the beginning."

So maybe I'm just now reaching my prime. Maybe God is not finished with me yet. Perhaps those years were not wasted; maybe the years were a time of training and development, God getting me ready to finish strong.

39

Good Men Lost

This is the story of some good men, good men who are lost. It's a story of three men who work hard, who love their families, who are fun to be with, and who are lost.

This is without a doubt the saddest thing I have to deal with in ministry to men – seeing good men I have grown up with, who I have shared my life with, ignore or rebel against God. Men who have so much potential and promise, yet will spend eternity in hell unless they come to know Jesus.

Barry (not his real name) made his fortune during the high tech boom. He is one of the funniest guys you will ever meet. Outwardly happy, carefree, and smart, Barry will have nothing to do with God. Any mention of church or the things of God brings a scowl and a closed mind.

Family is important to Barry. He adores his kids, loves his wife, and is generous with his time and his money. He's a good man who is lost.

Status, friends, and the next deal consume Barry's days. Golf, poker games, ski trips, football, and making money are the important things that drive him.

Kim (not his real name) is lost, but he does not know it. Kim came here from another county back in the 1970s. He learned English, taught himself a trade, and raised a family.

Soft-spoken, kind, and honest to the core, Kim is a joy to work with. I have never seen him angry or even frustrated. His self control and patience are a marvel to be experienced.

His character inspires loyalty and dedication in his employees and his skill and easy manner invokes respect and assurance from vendors and customers alike.

Kim is someone you would want your son to emulate. The example of an ideal brother, but Kim is lost.

The Bible was a part of Mack's (not his real name) early childhood. He attended a Christian school and a small country church. His mother prayed for him and would sometimes read him stories from the Bible.

Mack too loves his family and guards his grandkids from the culture vultures of our society, as any loving grandfather would.

Unlike Barry, Mack doesn't mind if you talk about spiritual things. He will listen to anyone on almost any spiritual topic, politely nod his head in agreement, and go about this life as if he never heard it.

Any of these men would give you the shirt off his back. They would get up at 2:00 a.m. and come out in a driving rainstorm to help you fix a broken down car or sit with you in the hospital if your wife was sick or dying.

These three good men and others like them keep me up at night. Like other men's ministry leaders, I have a burden for good men who are lost. Men who think their generosity, good works, or kind, gentle spirit will save them from God's final judgment.

Good men who are lost are why God has called me to men's ministry. There are over 63 million men in America who are lost. This is not acceptable. I will not stop as long as there are so many good men lost.

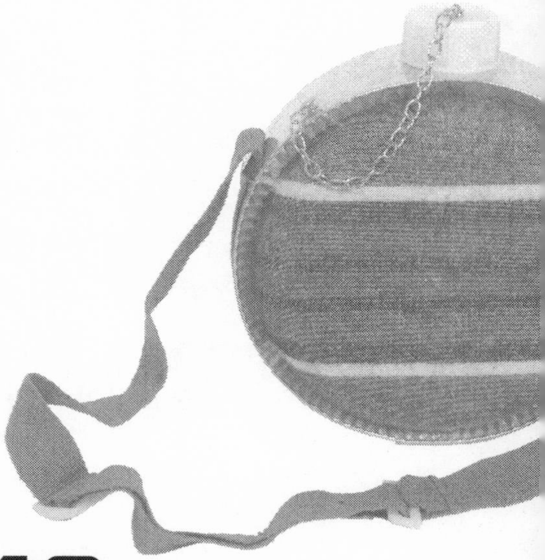

40 Adventure Quotes

1. "Are you weary of an ordinary existence? Your spiritual adventure awaits." *—John Eldredge*
2. "A man's heart needs beauty and adventure to come alive. Wilderness provides both; it is what pierces a man's heart." *—John Eldredge*
3. "God did not come to tame men, but to set them free." *—John Eldredge*
4. "There's an adventure waiting for you, a life you have been searching for." *—John Eldredge*
5. "Men are changed by what they experience more than by what they are told." *—David Murrow*

6. "A man just won't be happy until he's got adventure in his work, in his love, and in his spiritual life." *—John Eldredge*
7. "Most men live a dull existence in the flatlands." *—David Foster*
8. "Men, there is more out there for you, just over that next ridge, just around that next bend in the river." *—David Foster*
9. "Nature is a powerful tool for witnessing to the unchurched." *—John Eldredge*
10. "Men long to be challenged, pushed to their limits, to see just how far we can go, to be tested, physically, mentally, and spiritually." *—John Eldredge*
11. "Men were born to be wild, not born to be mild." *—David Foster*
12. "Adventure has value in spiritual formation." *—John Eldredge*
13. "God is present in His creation." *—David Murrow*
14. "Join an adventure that will last an eternity." *—Michael Tison*
15. "Do you want to be men of rugged faith or 'evanjellyfish' with no spiritual backbone?" *—Jack Ward*
16. "Our goal is to move men from exploring Christ to Christ-centeredness." *—unknown*
17. "Transformation of hearts and minds is not easy, it will be resisted and opposed...there is a war going on right now for possession of your heart. It is a subtle, tactical war fought

in the shadows and back thoughts of a mind distracted and a heart divided." *—David Foster*

18. "God can use a simple tool like me to impact the world, when we are weak, God gets the glory." *—Max Lucado*
19. "Be the Rock'n' Role. Be a strong, rugged leader for your family, be a Rock, and be a gentle hero, a good example, a Role model to your kids. Be the Rock'n'Role." *—unknown*
20. "Don't shuffle along with the herd, refuse to be tamed...stay Wild at heart. Don't let anyone tag you as mediocre." *—David Foster*

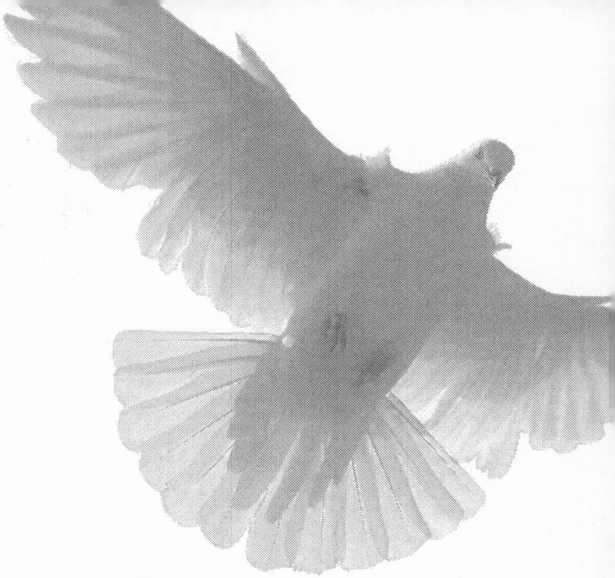

41
Holy Spirit

I don't know much about the Holy Spirit. I do know the Bible has a lot to say about him, but I must have skipped over it.

After living 35 years as a Christian I now feel compelled to know Him. I want the power and the wisdom that comes with an intimate, moment-by-moment relationship with the Holy Spirit. I ask the Lord to please forgive me for ignoring this part of who He is.

In his book *The Forgotten God,* Francis Chan points out that there is a direct correlation between the fact that most Christians have ignored the Holy Spirit and the ongoing feeling of dissatisfaction many have with the church and the lack of spiritual power in their lives.

Over the past few months I have begun to develop a bedtime routine of talking to the Holy Spirit. As a lay my head on my pillow, I have made an intentional effort to reach out to the Holy Spirit. Not to God, not to Jesus, not to the Lord. I address my comments to the Holy Spirit.

I'm not even certain this exercise is scriptural, this praying to the Holy Spirit. All I know is it's my attempt to connect with the part of God in the Bible that led Christians to do supernatural things.

Men, we need the power that comes from the Holy Spirit. I'm tired of trying to do ministry under my own power. Tired of allowing my sinful desires and misplaced passions to control my thoughts and my actions. Tired of ignoring the nudge the Holy Spirit gives throughout the day. Tired of the missed opportunities to follow the God of the universe to places he wants to take me.

Late at night, before I close my eyes, I have started to ask the Holy Spirit to speak godly virtue into my life.

I'll say something like, "Lord, tonight while I'm sleeping, plant in my heart, the Fruits of the Spirit: love, joy, peace, patience, kindness, goodness, and faithfulness."

I normally add a few others like wisdom and forgiveness because I'm a heavy sleeper and the Holy Spirit has got all night to do his work in my life.

I also ask the Holy Spirit to remove any ungodly habits like anger, bitterness, greed, lust, and other negative actions, and to replace them with the gifts of the spirit.

Some nights I may be too tired and forget, but I am developing this habit, and I look forward to this intimate time with the

Holy Spirit.

If God is in the wind, if God is actively working in this world, as I believe he is, then he is in my subconscious while I sleep. The seven or eight hours that I am not aware of Him or anything else, the Holy Spirit is actively working to mold me into a likeness of the Father.

42
Transformers

Men, we must do more than change. We can't settle for change. Change is everywhere, remember, hope and change, change and hope. We change constantly; we change jobs, change houses, change churches, and change wives.

To change is a choice. Deuteronomy 30:15-20 says, "I set before you today life and death, blessing and the curse...choose!" That sounds like more than a simple act of trying on something new. "Choose life or death." It's your choice and it's more than change, its transformation.

Here's how the American Heritage Dictionary defines the word transformed: "To change markedly, to take on the form of another, to change ones nature, function, or condition, to convert. Transforming is the mapping or the tracing of one space onto another."

We will be "markedly" different; our lives will be a sign that we are different. As plain as bold print on a blank page, we will be marked for the world to see.

When we are transformed we take on a new nature, more loving and more forgiving. Our function is now different. Where we once lived for self, we now have a holy function, a purpose and a meaning greater than self.

Our condition is changed. A once soul-sick human is now transformed into a dynamic, heart healthy, spiritual being, healed by the presence of the Great Physician and fit for eternity.

To be transformed is to be re-created into the image of the Almighty. It's as if we have been held up next to Him and the Holy Spirit has traced His image onto ours. It's as if the design of His DNA has been mapped onto us.

James Macdonald says, "The job of transformation is ours and the Lord's; our willingness and His power." Change is not enough. Transformation is required. We must be in His shadow, in His steps. We will fit like a glove into His image.

In his book *Finding Your Greater Yes,* Dr. Dan Erickson makes note of how we are transformed: through an intimate encounter with God, through His Word, through prayer, by yielding to the Holy Spirit, and by the renewing of our minds.

God's transforming power is a miracle to behold. I have seen men who are totally self-absorbed, arrogant, and prideful be transformed into humble servants who put others first and who love like Jesus loved.

When men who were once obsessed with power, money, and sex become controlled by the Spirit, their lives are transformed. People are no longer just objects to be manipulated, money is no longer an idol to be worshiped, and sex isn't recreation but a special gift from God.

43
The Way

The Ozark Mountains are crisscrossed with steep roads and trails. Some are only short turn-outs and off-shoots of the main trail and end after a few hundred feet. Some are long loops that go up on the side of a hill or down into a hollow and then circle back into the main trail. Others can be a totally new trail that may run for miles before it dead-ends in the middle of nowhere.

As the leader of the Ridge-Runner ATV tours, it's my responsibility to make sure nobody gets lost and everyone gets back safely. Part of my instructions to each group includes a stern warning to wait for the guy behind you whenever we turn off the main trail.

What invariably happens is the main body of riders makes a left turn and some of the stragglers at the rear make a right turn.

We may not notice that we have lost a rider until we get to the next stop. I must stop and do a head count of riders and realize that someone has missed the turn.

Some religions will tell you that there are many ways to heaven. We are all on a different path to God. You've got your trail and I have mine, they will say. The Bible clearly teaches that Jesus is the only way to heaven that no one comes to the Father except through the Son.

You may be sincere in your belief that all religions are equal, but if you take a wrong turn, sincere or not, you are lost. At every turn there are those that say, turn here, follow me, this way is smoother. Don't be a straggler; stay with the leader. Jesus is the way to the Father. There's no other way to God; don't miss Him.

Whenever a rider has missed the turn, we have to wait for him or risk sending someone back to find him. The whole group is affected when one member misses the turn. Sometimes it's more than one rider who misses the turn. A failure to follow the leader and a failure to wait on the guys behind you can cause one after another to miss the main trail.

Don't miss the trail. It affects not only your life, but those who follow you. Focus on Jesus, the leader of your life. Stay in His shadow, follow His lead, move when He moves, and turn when He turns. There is no other way that leads home.

I realize that it is not politically correct to say that there is only one way to heaven. The Bible clearly states that the way to the Father is through His son Jesus Christ.

44
Adventure in God's Word!

Job 12:7–12... "Ask the animals, the birds, the fish...they will tell you that the hand of the Lord made this."

Psalm 42:1... "As the deer pants for the water, so my soul longs for you."

Psalm 24:1... "The earth is the Lord's, and all it contains."

Mark 4:41... "How can this be that even the wind and the waves obey Him?"

Isaiah 40:31... "Those who wait upon the Lord will gain new strength; they will mount up with wings like eagles."

Jeremiah 29:1... "I know the plans I have for you, declares the Lord, plans for your welfare and not for calamity, to give you a future and a hope."

Psalm 19:1... "The heavens declare the glory of the Lord."

Psalm 147:4... "He counts the stars and calls them by name."

Proverbs 3:6... "He will direct your paths."

John 14:6... "I am the way."

Psalm 37:5... "Commit your way to the Lord."

II Corinthians 2:15–16... "You are the aroma of Christ to the world."

45
Anger

Most men have a problem with anger. It's a fact. I have seen it, I have experienced it, and our wives and kids tell us it's there.

Ever been tail-gated by a red pick-up truck full of road rage? Witnessed a dad berate his kids in the produce aisle? Been embarrassed by an out-of-control boss who screams at the innocent UPS driver?

Anger impacts your relationship with others. Your wife, your kids, your co-workers, your friends – everyone in your life is impacted by your anger.

Some men explode at the slightest irritation they face, while others may not show it, but the anger is always there, just under the surface, ready to boil over.

Your body is feeling the impact of your constant anger. You were not designed to live with a constant adrenaline drip. Physically you will pay a high price for your anger. Doctors tell us that high blood pressure, heart disease, and stroke are all related to the stress that accompanies anger.

Many men are emotionally isolated. Anger impacts their emotional lives and plays a major role in this isolation. Know this, when everyone else is always wrong, when you blame others for your problems, when your attitude is more like the world than like Christ, you have a problem with anger.

Not only are you impacted physically and emotionally by your anger, but anger also impacts your spiritual life. Your relationship with God is affected by your anger toward people.

Anger can be an obstacle to opportunities to be used by God. He is more interested in your character than in your abilities. Anger will prevent you from reaching the potential and promise that God has for your life.

Anger can impact how you represent God to others. People may feel you think too highly of yourself when you are always frustrated and irritable with others.

Pastor Wes George of First Baptist Church of Rogers, Arkansas lists five keys to dealing with anger. First, we must understand grace. If you feel entitled and put yourself ahead of others, you probably don't understand the concept of grace.

Grace says you are entitled to nothing. Grace says we all deserve eternal damnation. Only through the grace of God are we able to enjoy the abundant life that God offers us.

Second, you must experience forgiveness if you want to deal with your anger. Realize that God died for you and has forgiven you of all past, present, and future sins.

Third, you must express forgiveness to others. Just as God has forgiven you, you too must forgive those who have hurt you. This is a key element to dealing with your anger.

Fourth is to avoid people, places, and situations that make you angry. You must do your part to stay away from those people and things that cause your blood to boil.

The final key to dealing with your anger is to find your purpose in life. God has designed each of you with a special combination of talents, gifts, and skills that no one else has. When you find your purpose, you will come to realize that life is not about you, it's all about Jesus.

46
On Ramp... Off Ramp

News junkies and political animals will remember "The Bridge to Nowhere," a 2004 attempt by some in Congress to build a 1.3 mile bridge from Ketchikan, Alaska to the 50 residents of Gravina Island. The proposed $400 million project became the laughingstock of citizens who oppose government waste, and to Christians, a vivid description of life without God.

A bridge to nowhere is exactly what many men are building when they focus on a life built on material things and selfish ambitions. Because of the need to succeed and constant pressure to have more, it's nearly impossible to get off this road to riches that our society tells us is so important.

To the neglect of their families, their health, and their spiritual growth, many men spend 60-hour work weeks trying to get onto a bridge that leads to nowhere – no satisfaction, no lasting peace of mind, and no way off.

I want to introduce you to a "Bridge to Somewhere." This bridge spans the moat of our sinful culture and is a bridge that leads to an island of treasure.

In order to access this bridge you must first get on the right road. Think of the cross as the bridge that leads from spiritual death to eternal life. Rugged Faith

Ministries is here to serve as a "ramp" to the cross, to point men that may not know the Lord to the "On Ramp" and help those guys who have accepted Christ, but are not currently following Him, to the "Off Ramp."

A bridge connects two points. Rugged Faith wants to help move men from a sinfully destructive life to a life of peace and purpose that only comes when they accept the fact that Jesus loved them enough to die on the cross for their sins.

Most bridges cross natural obstacles like water, ravines, and swamps. The cross is the only bridge that can help men conquer things like greed, lust, bitterness, and all the other deadly obstacles that keep them from reaching the Promised Land.

When considering the On Ramp you should follow these four important steps; watch for the signs, check behind you, slow down, and yield.

First, watch for signs. Have you noticed that your life is not what it should be? When you look in the mirror, do you see someone you don't like very much? Is there something inside telling you to stop, to turn from the life you are now living? Do you realize that you have been living life so fast you have forgotten what's really important?

We try to watch and listen to men who come to our Rugged Faith events. We want to hear what is on their hearts, to learn what they are thinking. We watch for signs they are open to the message of the cross, and we get to observe how God transforms them right before our eyes.

I encourage you to watch for signs as you go through your day. Ask God to give you spiritual antennae to pick up signals from the hurting people He puts in your path.

Second, maybe you need to check behind you and see where you have been and who is following you. If you are a Christian, it's important to remember where you came from and see how far God has brought you.

If you are not a Christian you also need to look behind you, not to beat yourself up for all your mistakes, but to evaluate how you have spent your life thus far. We only have a limited number of days on this earth. Have you wasted much of your life so far? Do you want more out of life?

You should also look behind you because many of you have sons and daughters who are following you. Are you living the kind of life that is a good example to them, or are you leading them into the same mistakes you made?

Finally, you must be willing to slow down and yield your agenda and trust God that the way of the cross is what's best for you. To yield is to give God permission to direct your life.

The combination of economic stress and rapid cultural change has brought many men to a spiritual crossroads in their lives, and to a time of decision. You have a choice to make. Will you continue a life of excess and materialism that keeps you in the rat race, or will you look for an exit to something better?

Whenever you come to a crossroads you are forced to make a decision. It was Yogi Berra who said, "When you come to a fork in the road, take it." Many men have considered Christ, but have never made a decision to accept Him. Others have given their

lives to Christ but have never grown into the kind of men God wants them to be. Both find themselves at a spiritual crossroads.

This is where we come in; Rugged Faith Ministries wants to assist men at the crossroads of life. We want to be the simple, humble, crossing attendant who helps men exit a life controlled by the world, and get onto a bridge to somewhere.

Men of all ages are looking for something that only God can provide. If Rugged Faith can serve as an "On Ramp" or an "Off Ramp" to men at the crossroads of life, we can reach our stated goals to guide, prepare, and support.

Hopefully this diagram will give you a clearer understanding of the On Ramp, Off Ramp concept.

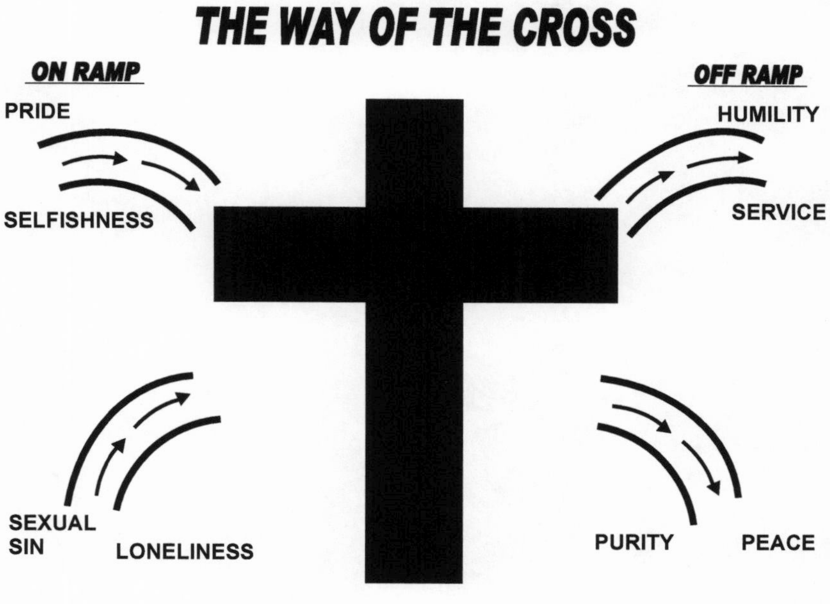
THE WAY OF THE CROSS
ON RAMP
OFF RAMP
PRIDE
SELFISHNESS
HUMILITY
SERVICE
SEXUAL SIN
LONELINESS
PURITY
PEACE

47
Make a Plan

You cannot do everything at once, but you can do something at once. You just need a map.

For our purposes, "map" is an acrinym. M.A.P. stands for **M**ake **A P**lan.

Studies show that only 5% of people have a written out their "Life Plan / Goals." Those 5% who do reach their goals 95% of the time. Those who have nothing planned, often achieve... nothing.

Using the chart on the next page (or one like it), list two or three goals for each category for each time limit. Make this your plan.

	Short Term 1 day – 6 mo.	Mid Term 6 mo. – 3 yrs.	Long Term 3 yrs. – 10 yrs.
Personal			
Family & Marriage			
Church / Spiritual			
Financial			
Bucket List			

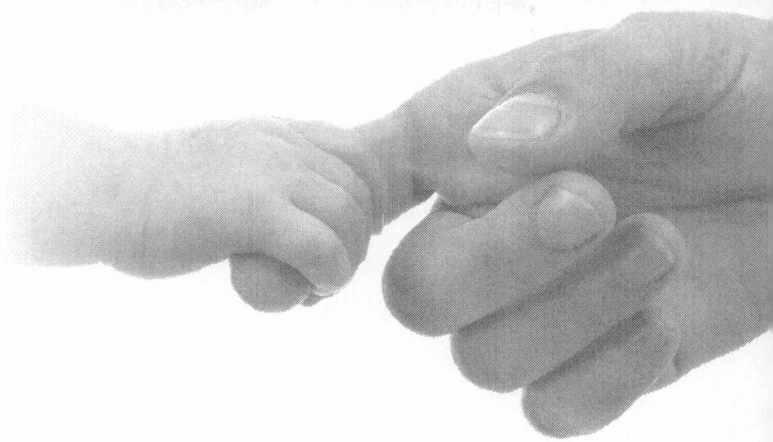

48
Taken

I recently watched the movie *Taken*. It is the story of a father who goes up against seemingly impossible odds to rescue his daughter who has been kidnapped and sold into the sex trade.

Even through the story is violent and the language is a little rough, I found it very entertaining and to have an important lesson for Christians.

One of the final scenes is the successful rescue of the daughter. After the danger has passed and she realizes that her father has saved her, she says with stunned astonishment, "Daddy, you came for me."

This scene is a vivid picture of humans when we come to the realization that God, our heavenly father, has come to save us from sin and death. The idea that almighty God would go through hell and back to save a black-hearted sinner like me is astonishing.

In the movie, a wounded and bruised father replies with equal astonishment, “I told you I would.” Throughout the Bible God tells us that He has come to seek and save those who are lost. If just one sheep is missing, He goes out to find and rescue the lost.

I recommend this movie to all men. It is a story of courage, determination, and love, three traits of a godly man.

49
Solid Rock

Solid Rock began in 1989 in Southern California. Pastor Chuck Smith at Calvary Chapel in Costa Mesa helped fund the new ministry. The first events were held in Yosemite National Park.

When the struggling ministry to climbers was less than a year old the founder, Dan Freeman, was killed in a biking accident.

With the help of volunteers, the ministries continued and grew in spurts throughout the 1990's. Calvin Landrus worked as a volunteer during much of that time.

In 2002 while working as an associate pastor, Calvin felt God was calling him to serve as full-time director of Solid Rock.

When Calvin asked his wife, "How about a new ministry to

climbers?" she said, "No way, you are just looking for an excuse to go climbing."

Calvin and his wife re-birthed Solid Rock where it began, in Yosemite. They had a spaghetti supper for about 100 climbers and shared the vision for the ministry.

Today the ministry is thriving with Landrus as the director.

Calvin is 48 years old, about 6 feet tall and 175 pounds. He keeps in shape by climbing the rocks near his home in Bend, Oregon and by using the indoor climbing wall during bad weather.

Calvin says because of his experience, he is a better climber today than ever before. He has climbed Half Dome and El Capitán in Yosemite plus numerous other famous rocks across the U.S.

Landrus has climbed with Doug Englekirk, one of the premier rock climbers in the world. Calvin was with Doug when he "free climbed" El Capitán with no climbing aids.

A typical climb of El Capitán can take up to five days and requires climbers to drag 120 pounds of water, food, and supplies behind them in a haul bag.

Climbing and sharing the Gospel with other climbers are the two passions of Calvin's life.

Landrus tells the story of fellow climber John Dargis, whose shirt was caught in his billet device. In the attempt to cut his shirt free, he cut the rope as well. Thankfully, just moments before, he had clipped onto a safety line and was saved from a fall to his death.

Calvin tells another story of the same climber. While in Alaska, he fell into an ice crevasse and was almost killed. The same year Dargis was lost in a white-out on the mountain. After these three near death experiences, Dargis gave his life to the Lord.

"The mountain makes us aware of the fact that there is something beyond ourselves, something far greater that only God could have made," says Calvin.

Obstacles that many climbers face to "conquer the rock" include fear of falling, fear of failure, and peer pressure.

You must conquer the fear within you. Your must learn to trust your training, trust your gear, and most importantly, trust your climbing partner.

When you are on the mountain you must have complete trust in your climbing partner. Calvin says this time on the mountain gives him a unique opportunity to share his faith.

One obstacle to faith for a climber is his own God-given ability. This self-made, I-did-it attitude is common and tends to prevent climbers from seeking after God. A false sense of "I can do anything, I don't need God" is hard to overcome in successful climbers.

Solid Rock Climbers for Christ is reaching out to climbers with a newsletter and wants to include Camp Fire Forums where climbers can share the experiences and share their faith.

50
Purpose

A prominent author recently said, "Meaning is the new money." I'm not sure I would go that far, but it's true the men are searching for meaning as never before in my lifetime.

Perhaps it's the threat of financial collapse our nation is facing, the uncertainty of the future, or ever-rising unemployment. Purpose is the new paycheck that an ever-growing number of men yearn for.

Chuck Swindoll says, "We were not thrown on this earth like dice tossed across a table. We were lovingly placed here with a purpose."

This "thunderstorm of purpose," as author Daniel Pink calls it, is beginning to roar across our society as more and more of the nation's 78 million Baby Boomers near age 60.

Without a cause, many men live out bored, unfulfilled lives in the search of significance. Frustrated, bitter, and lonely, men never seem content without a mountain to climb.

“These feelings are from God,” says Pat Morley, in his book *Pastoring Men*. “He has placed this longing for purpose in men’s hearts so they will seek Him.”

Would you give up your current salary, or a portion of it, in exchange for a more meaningful career? Studies show that six out of ten men are dissatisfied with their jobs.

Would you be willing to move to another state or county to join a cause you felt strongly about?

In a culture in which materialism is the mortar that holds our nation together, more and more men are answering a resounding YES to these questions.

A cause, a mission, meaning, purpose, significance or whatever you want to call it is in great demand. If we as ministry leaders can guide men to a deeper understanding of their God-given purpose, men will follow.

51
Culp

The white, three-story structure looks like a box. It's perched on a slight incline in a stand of old growth pines. A narrow, gravel driveway leads up to and encircles the lonesome country schoolhouse known simply as Culp.

Hardy Mennonite missionaries came to this part of the Ozarks in the 1940s and started the school and a church they called Bethel Springs.

My brothers and I all attended the Culp School through the sixth grade, when we then had to transfer to the public school across the river in Calico Rock.

The formative years I spent at this country school still serve me well today. The simple things of life mean more. The discipline I learned is a continued blessing, and the friendships and memories made there will stay with me forever.

Other than my mother and father, the first person of influence in my life was my first grade teacher, Miss Mae. I can still remember her stern but kind voice and the sound the chalk made on the old blackboard as she called students to the front to solve math problems.

Miss Mae, like many others, poured their lives into mine and made me what I am today. Too many times we fail to acknowledge those who contributed to the person we are today. The knowledge imparted, the values transmitted, the example modeled, and things experienced all come together with inherited traits in the making of a man.

As I look back over my fifty-something years I thank God for people God has sent into my life; A praying mother, a godly wife, loving in-laws, wise teachers, strong men, trained spiritual leaders, common sense brothers, and a cast of unknown Christians and guardian angels.

Miss Mae taught me how to read and gave me a love of books and a hunger for knowledge. She told me that JFK had been shot and that Jesus had died for my sins. She wiped my face when I was sick and challenged me to always do better.

Today the Culp School is used by the Mennonite church and is called Calvary Bible School. Young men and women from across the country come to my little school in the pines for spiritual training and emotional renewal.

I will always have fond memories of my years at Culp. The big swing in the back of the school, building a snow fort, the daily chapel services, and Christmas programs all seem like another lifetime.

I was fortunate enough to see Miss Mae a few years ago. She was 87 years old and has since passed away. She had written a small book about her years as a teacher at Culp School. In the cover of my copy she had written the following: "Keep walking with the Lord-He is faithful and has a beautiful home prepared for you when your work on earth is done... Praise His name!"

It's a special blessing to have people of influence like Miss Mae pour their lives into ours. May you and I become such influencers.

52
Bill

The old VW bug slips and slides through the wet red clay of soon to be Arkansas Highway Five. The overnight rain has left the new roadbed impassable for most motorists.

Yellow road graders and bulldozers sit quietly by as Bill slides to a stop and guns the engine of the little car that can.

"You think we should try it?" asks my brother Lynn. "I don't think we can make it, that hill's pretty steep," I yell from the back seat.

Bill just grins as he slaps the mud buggy into reverse. "I'll get a run at it. We can make it."

We move backwards to a level dry area and stop. "Hang on, here she goes!" Bill screams as he floorboards the bug and we hurtle toward the steep mud monster of a hill.

With red clay flying we bounce and spin and yell as the little rear engine rig shoots over the crest of hill, narrowly missing a flashing Road Closed sign.

We pull over to look back at the "impassable" hill and laugh. In the pitch black of November we see the headlights of another vehicle at the bottom of the hill.

"They will never make it in that pick-up truck," Lynn says. "I tell you what; let's see if the key is in that tractor over there."

Bill jumps in the seat of the big highway department tractor, starts it up, and yells, "We will give them a tow!"

The rest of the night is spent chaining and towing stranded motorists up the muddy hill, in return for a small fee, of course. Not a bad night's wages, considering we were using the state's equipment.

My early teen years are filled with wonderful experiences with my two older brothers and our friend Billy Joe. Almost like a member of the family, Bill spent about as much time at our house as he did at his own.

Exploring caves, building tree houses, fishing, hunting, and camping, we spent much of our waking hours in the outdoors. We never knew we were poor and seldom tired of each other's company.

Boulder Bill lived a few miles down the road at the foot of Boulder Mountain. He was a great storyteller and could spin a yarn with the best of them. We never knew when he was lying or telling the truth. His stories had such vivid details we didn't really care.

A lifelong resident of Stone County, Bill is a blast from the past.

He talks slow, is always genuine, and would walk across hell and back to help my brothers and me. He is true friend, a brother by another mother.

The world says friendships like that of David and Jonathan in the Old Testament are impossible today. Because many men are superficial and plastic with their buddies, they never have true, deep friendships.

Many men stay alone at the bottom, not risking a run at the hill, believing that it's too hazardous to get close to people. They spend their days frustrated and lonely with few real friends.

When the world warns you that the road to friendship is impassable, you don't believe it. If you don't have a friend like Bill in your life, I encourage you to start now. Men need the strong, loyal friendship of other men.

Kenny Luck says, "Men are made in the company of other men." A dog is not man's best friend, a man is.

Notes

Special thanks to the following individuals and ministries who have contributed to this book.

1. Pat Morley... *No Man Left Behind* and *Pastoring Men*
2. Steve Sonderman... *How to Build a Life Changing Men's Ministry* and *Mobilizing Men for one-on-one Ministry*
3. Brian Doyle... Iron Sharpens Iron Ministries. Hartford, CT
4. Robert Lewis... *Men's Fraternity*
5. Erwin McManus... *Chasing Daylight*
6. David Murrow... *Why Men Hate Going to Church*
7. Chip Ingram... *Good to Great in God's Eyes*

8. David Foster... *Accept No Mediocre Life*
9. Phil Downer... *Effective Men's Ministry*
10. John Eldredge... *Wild at Heart*
11. Steve Farrar... *God Built*
12. Kenny Luck... *Risk*
13. Francis Chan... *The Forgotten God* and *Crazy Love*
14. Jim Collins... *Good to Great*
15. Bill Peel... *What God Does When Men Lead*
16. Ray Vander Laan... *Echoes of His Presence*
17. Andy Stanley... *Visioneering*
18. Doug Munton... *Heroes in Hiding*
19. Daniel Pink... *A Whole New Mind*
20. Paul Coughlin... *No More Christian Nice Guy*
21. Craig Groeschel... *It*
22. George Barna... *Revolution*
23. John MacArthur... *12 Ordinary Men*
24. Dan Erickson... *Finding Your Greater Yes*
25. Bruce Wilkinson... *You were Born for This*
26. John Quincey Woolf... *Life in the Leatherwoods*
27. Paul David Tripp... *Broken Down Church*
28. Mark Driscoll... *Vintage Jesus*

About the Author

Jack Ward is the founder and CEO of Rugged Faith Ministries. His Rugged Faith Boot Camps and Iron Sharpens Iron National Men's Conferences have been attended by hundreds of men. He speaks and writes on topics of interest to men, and has developed "MML-101" a Seminar for Men's Ministry Leaders. Jack and his wife Brenda live in Springdale, Arkansas. To learn more, visit his web site at www.ruggedfaith.net

7500440R0

Made in the USA
Charleston, SC
11 March 2011